MASONIC TRIALS

AND

MICHIGAN DIGEST:

A TREATISE UPON THE

Law and Practice of Masonic Trials,

WITH FORMS AND PRECEDENTS.

CONTAINING ALSO

A DIGEST OF THE DECISIONS OF THE GRAND MASTERS OF MICHIGAN, APPROVED BY THE GRAND LODGE; THE RESOLUTIONS, ORDERS AND EDICTS, CONSTITUTION AND BY-LAWS OF THE GRAND LODGE; A HISTORY OF THE GRAND LODGE OF MICHIGAN; A COMPLETE ROLL OF GRAND OFFICERS, FROM THE ORGANIZATION OF THE GRAND LODGE TO THE PRESENT TIME; THE ANCIENT LANDMARKS, ANCIENT CONSTITUTIONS, CHARGES AND REGULATIONS, AND AN APPENDIX OF GENERAL FORMS.

BY HENRY M. LOOK,

Past Master; G. V. and L. of Michigan; K. T.

PONTIAC, MICH.:

PRESS OF RANN & TURNER, GAZETTE OFFICE.

1869.

ERRATA.—On page 81, seventh line from the top, for "*sentence,*" read *decision.*

On page 158, bottom line, for "*reject,*" read *recommend.*

TO THE

MOST WORSHIPFUL GRAND LODGE

OF

FREE AND ACCEPTED MASONS

OF THE

STATE OF MICHIGAN,

I

DEDICATE THIS VOLUME

AS A

MARK OF ESTEEM FOR ITS INDIVIDUAL MEMBERS,

OF

GRATITUDE FOR ITS FAVOR AND SUPPORT,

AND OF

VENERATION FOR THOSE SUBLIME PRINCIPLES

WHICH IT HAS

ALWAYS

STEADFASTLY MAINTAINED.

PREFACE.

In presenting to the Masonic fraternity a treatise upon the LAW AND PRACTICE OF MASONIC TRIALS, I have attempted to supply what every intelligent craftsman has long felt to be an absolute *necessity*. Established system is everywhere necessary; and especially is it essential in the administration of justice. To aid in securing this most important result in the adjudication of Masonic causes, and to systematize, to some extent, the modes of practice and procedure in Masonic tribunals, is the object of this volume. By a general adherence to a uniform practice in the conduct of trials in subordinate lodges, a majority of the appeals which annually go up to the Grand Lodge, to engross its time and encumber its records, would undoubtedly be prevented; for by far the greater number of them are made for irregularity in practice, and not upon the merits.

The FORMS given in this work constitute one of its most important features. They have been prepared with much care, and have been made to conform to the most reliable precedents, except where the former rule has been changed by subsequent enactments; in which case they have been adapted to the legislation of our Grand Lodge as now in force.

The MICHIGAN DIGEST, which follows the treatise upon Masonic Trials, comprehends all the settled and important written legislation of this jurisdiction, with the decisions of the Grand Masters and the rulings of the Grand Lodge in the most important cases. By thus for the first time placing our local law in the hands of the craft in a convenient and orderly form, I trust I have contributed somewhat to their convenience and profit, as well as lightened in some measure the arduous labors of the Grand Masters, whose patience is so often tried by the constant repetition of questions that are already well settled.

The History of our Grand Lodge, and the Roll of Grand Officers, have been prepared with especial reference to exactness of detail.

The Ancient Landmarks, Constitutions, and Charges, I have deemed an essential adjunct to a work of this nature.

Soon after the preparation of this volume was begun, I learned that Past Grand Master S. C. Coffinbury was contemplating a similar work. I immediately, with a view of perfecting a mutual understanding, opened a correspondence with him, in the course of which I said to him, that my respect for his greater age and attainments prompted me to leave the adjustment of the matter entirely to him, and that I should yield a cheerful conformity to his wishes, however he might decide. To this he responded with a courtesy and magnanimity which I take pride in recording:

"I most cheerfully surrender to you the field. You are comparatively young: I am closing a life, and have preformed my part, as well as I could, in the Order. I could not reconcile myself in interposing obstacles in the way of your laudable efforts. Therefore proceed with your publication, and may success attend it."

Upon this I continued my labors; but I should be ungrateful if I failed here to properly acknowledge that kindness of spirit and nobleness of heart which have touched not me alone, but all the craft; which have cheered so often the social circle, brightened the mystic bonds of fraternity, and shone with no borrowed lustre from the Oriental Chair.

My acknowledgements are due to Grand Master A. T. Metcalf, for many valuable suggestions; to Grand Secretary James Fenton, for his kindness in placing at my disposal the records of the Order, and his patient assistance in searching their more difficult portions; to P. G. H. P. Cudworth, for many ancient works and documents; and to various distinguished brethren for numerous other Masonic and literary favors.

The principal works which have been consulted are those of Oliver, Morris, Mackey, Pike, Chase, Mitchell, Lockwood, Webb, and Sickels, and the minutes of the principal Grand Lodges.

And now into your hands, my Brethren, I commit the fruit of a season of pleasant labor, with the hope that that labor shall prove to have been not altogether in vain. Some of the subjects here treated are surrounded with peculiar difficulties. To assume that they have all been handled without error, would be to claim what no mortal ever yet achieved. I only ask for this volume such favorable judgment as you shall deem, after impartial examination, it justly merits. I especially request that you will not base your opinion upon a few detached paragraphs, or a single chapter, but judge of it as a whole. The arch is never complete until the key-stone is in place; and no book can be properly judged until its last chapter is read, and compared with all that precedes it, that the complete idea of the writer may appear.

HENRY M. LOOK.

PONTIAC, November 22d, 1869.

CONTENTS.

MASONIC TRIALS.

MICHIGAN DIGEST.

MASONIC TRIALS.

PRELIMINARY CHAPTER.

This work is not designed as a commentary upon the general system of Masonic Jurisprudence, but upon a particular department of that system. It is to the *Law of Masonic Offenses*, and of *Practice and Procedure in Masonic Trials*, that the author will confine his present inquiries; and in this field he designs to be as concise as shall be consistent with thoroughness. As incident to the main subject, he must necessarily treat of all those principles, rules, forms and proceedings which relate to the Offense, the Tribunal, the Trial and the Punishment.

While a multitude of books have been written upon Masonic Law,, the subject of *Masonic Trials* has never been treated in detail. The powers of Lodges and of Grand Lodges, the prerogatives of Masters and Wardens, the qualifications of candidates, and all questions of executive and legislative policy, have been elaborately and ably considered, while this vastly important and interesting department has been scarcely touched. It has generally been disposed of in a single chapter, occupying, in some instances, but a single page.

As a consequence, the most painful uncertainty and confusion have prevailed in the conduct of Masonic trials. No settled system of practice and procedure has been adhered to, for the reason that there has been no systematic treatise upon the subject. Yet there is no portion of our system upon which more vital interests depend than this, for upon the proper administration of Masonic justice, hang the honor and well-being of the Order. To this end a full understanding of the nature and definition of Masonic offenses is not alone necessary; settled rules of practice and procedure, and well defined forms and precedents, as well as a knowledge of the rules of evidence, and methods of proof, are also required.

It is therefore with a view to systematize, in some degree, our Masonic Judiciary, by placing in the hands of the craft a convenient book of reference in this regard, that this treatise is undertaken. No attempt will be made to press the individual opinions of the author, except as they shall be sustained by established law and usage. No principle or rule will be asserted except upon authority of the ablest authors, or the decision of the highest Masonic tribunals. To collect, collate, and reduce to some definite form and order that learning which is now floating here and there in indiscriminate fragments, will be the main object of the writer.

The subject naturally falls into the following order, and will accordingly be so treated, viz:

1. Of the Offense.
2. Of the Tribunal.
3. Of the Jurisdiction.
4. Of the Charges.
5. Of the Answer.
6. Of the Proofs.
7. Of the Argument.
8. Of the Deliberation.
9. Of the Judgment.
10. Of the Penalty.
11. Of Appeals.
12. Of New Trials.
13. Of Restoration.
14. Of Grand Lodge Trials.

All the forms necessary to be used in the course of Masonic trials are inserted in their appropriate connection in the body of the work. The advantage of their being thus placed in immediate relation to the text will, it is believed, be apparent to every one.

I.

OF THE OFFENSE.

Every violation, by a Mason, of his Masonic obligations, or of the established laws, usages and customs of the fraternity, every violation of the moral law, and every violation of the municipal law involving moral turpitude, is a Masonic offense, for which the offender may, upon due conviction, be subjected to such lawful punishment as the tribunal having jurisdiction in the case shall adjudge.

But Masonry will not take cognizance of those offenses which are merely ecclesiastical or political in their nature, because, as an institution, she ignores all sectarian opinions and controversies, and all questions of state policy. She recognizes every *de facto* government, gives the freest latitude to partisan and political sentiment, and dwells a peaceful subject under the flag of every civilized nation upon earth. She accords the same freedom to every man's religious opinions, so long as he acknowledges the existence and sovereignty of God, and yields a practical obedience to the moral law; *but that limit he must not pass*, under penalty of banishment from the Order.

Therefore heresy, schism, and apostasy, are not Masonic offenses, unless they amount to a violation of one or more of the three great duties which a Mason owes to his God, his neighbor and himself. Neither are treason and rebellion, in and of themselves, subjects of Masonic discipline, for the reason that they are of a purely political character. Unless they also involve *moral turpitude*, the Masonic jurisdiction will not attach. It was this principle, which has been so long settled and so universally adhered to, that saved from dissolution the lodges of England, France and Germany, during their intestine struggles, and the various Colonial lodges during the American Revolution. Otherwise every Mason in the United Colonies in 1776 would have been subject to expulsion, and every lodge to a forfeiture of its warrant by the Grand Lodges of England and Scotland, under whose jurisdiction they were at the time. The spirit of Freemasonry dwells in a region above and beyond the ambition of kings and the craft of politicians; in a region where mere forms of government are unheeded, where the wrangling of parties is not heard, and the sound of battle never comes. Yet disloyalty and rebellion are always to be discountenanced, and every mason is enjoined to "conform with cheerfulness to the government of the country in which he lives." (See the Ancient Charges of 1722, No. 2.)

Masonry will not take cognizance of a breach of

contract or agreement between a Mason and a profane, nor between one Mason and another, unless involving moral turpitude in the offender. Masonic tribunals do not assume to adjust mere legal rights.

A violation of the municipal law, or the law of the land, is a Masonic offense, provided it be *malum in se*, and not merely *malum prohibitum*—it must be an evil in itself, and not merely wrong because prohibited by law. For instance, murder, arson, assault, larceny, adultery, forgery and counterfeiting, are Masonic offenses, because they are not only violations of the municipal law, but are also evils in themselves. But a violation of the game laws, practicing a profession without license, or issuing unstamped notes or receipts, although in direct violation of the public statutes, are offenses of which Masonry will take no cognizance, for the reason that they are only *mala prohibita*.

Masonry punishes certain public crimes and misdemeanors, not because they are violations of the law of the land, but because they are violations of the law of Masonry. The Masonic tribunals do not assume, in any sense, to administer the public criminal code. Our Masonic Criminal Jurisprudence is based solely upon the peculiar laws and landmarks of the Masonic institution, and upon that sublime system of morality given by God Himself.

An attorney at law, who is a Mason, is not chargeable with unmasonic conduct if, in instituting proceedings against a brother, whether affiliant or non-affiliant, he fails to forewarn the brother of the same. He has no right to prejudice the lawful interests of his client, which might be the result in numerous cases, if the opposite rule should prevail. There is no rule of Masonic usage which prohibits a Mason, who is an attorney, from taking a fee and conducting a suit or prosecution against a brother Master Mason. A Master Mason is not bound, in any instance, to protect or shield a brother in wrong or dishonesty, especially not in crime. (Decisions of G. M. Nos. 50 and 79.)

The following are some (but by no means all) of the more flagrant Masonic offenses, viz:

All public crimes and misdemeanors involving moral turpitude.

Gambling and profligacy.

Drunkenness. (Const. of G. L., Art. 6, Sec. 13.)

Profanity and blasphemy.

Slander and backbiting.

Fighting and brawling.

Duelling.

Improper revelations.

Undue solicitations for candidates.

Over-zealous arguments with the enemies of Masonry.

Disobedience of superiors, or contemptuous language toward them.

Expression of contemptuous opinions of the institution of Masonry.

All countenance of impostors.

Masonic communion with clandestine Masons. (Const. of G. L., Art. 6, Sec. 16.)

Visiting irregular or clandestine lodges.

Unseemly conduct in the lodge.

Abuse of the ballot. (Decisions of G. M. No. 87.)

Malfeasance in office.

Defrauding or wronging a Mason, or a Masonic lodge.

Adultery, and all lascivious association, whether with the relative of a Master Mason, or with a stranger. (Decisions of G. M. No. 78.)

Any violation whatever of the technical parts or points of the several Masonic obligations.

Violation of the particular injunctions of the ritual, or of any of the Landmarks of Masonry.

Violation of the Constitution, laws, edicts, rules, by-laws or regulations of the Grand Lodge, or of a subordinate lodge by a member thereof.

Visiting, or attempting to visit, a lodge, while under sentence of suspension or expulsion.

Use of intoxicating liquors in lodge-rooms, or at lodge communications. (Const. of G. L., Art. 6, Sec. 14.)

Non-payment of dues.

Cruel treatment of wife, child, or other member of one's family.

Inhumanity to inferiors and dependents, whether Masons or not.

Contempt for God and religion.

Atheism.

Other particular Masonic offenses might be specified almost without limit, but the general rules and principles already laid down, with the various specifications given, will, we think, be sufficient to enable any brother having a tolerable knowledge of those fundamental ideas upon which our Masonic institution is based, to determine at once whether any given act is or is not a Masonic offense.

II.

OF THE TRIBUNAL.

None but a strictly Masonic tribunal can take judicial cognizance of a Masonic offense. The only judicial tribunals known in ancient craft Masonry, are Lodges and Grand Lodges. True, the Grand Master and the Worshipful Master have certain important prerogatives, some of them of a semi-judicial nature, which they may exercise when the regular body is not in session; but every act which either of them may perform in that behalf is subject to review by the body whose instrument they are. Neither of them is in any sense a *court.* He cannot *adjudicate;* he cannot try, sentence nor punish. Whatever action he may take in his single official capacity, as touching a *Masonic trial,* is only of a preliminary, incidental or interlocutory character. It does not and cannot reach the merits of the case. The ultimate judicial power rests only in the Lodge or the Grand Lodge.

A lodge must be regularly chartered and duly constituted, its officers elected and installed, and in all respects a regular working lodge, before it can hear or determine a Masonic trial. Lodges under dispensation have no judicial powers whatever. (Decisions of G. M., Nos. 44 and 68.)

Charges cannot be presented nor received, nor any proceedings taken in a Masonic trial at any other than a regular communication, and the lodge must be open upon the highest degree to which the accused has attained. The trial must begin at a regular communication; but after it is thus begun it may continue at special communications called for that purpose, which would, in such case, be considered only as a continuation of the regular. Some authors hold that the trial may begin at a special communication called for that purpose, but the weight of authority is in favor of the rule as above stated. (Res. of G. L., No. 23.)

The presence of visitors ought not to be permitted during any portion of a Masonic trial, and certainly not during the consideration and discussion of the charges.

The lodge, while sitting for the trial of a cause, is in every sense a judicial body, of which the Worshipful Master is the presiding head. No business of a general or legislative character should be introduced while the trial is under immediate consideration. Every *member of the lodge* in good standing is authorized to sit upon the trial, and ought to be present. While so sitting he should remember that he is acting, not in his ordinary Masonic capacity, but as one of a bench of judges. In his hands are placed, for the time being, the dearest and most vital interests of the accused, and every trace of prejudice or partiality should be banished from his breast until the case shall reach its final conclusion. If, on account of any deep personal interest in the case, or any peculiar enlistment of his passions, he thinks himself unable to hear and judge with the strictest impartiality, he should so state; and thereupon the lodge may, by vote, excuse him from sitting in the case.

The Worshipful Master presides at the trial, as at every other lodge proceeding. He has authority to decide all points of order, and all questions relating to the legality or regularity of any service, paper or proceeding in the case, to allow or forbid amendments and continuances, to admit or exclude evidence, and control debate. No appeal can be taken from his decision to the lodge, in case he shall rule erroneously, but he is responsible to the Grand Lodge for any abuse of these powers, as in all other cases. He may take the sense of the lodge as to each of the matters aforesaid, if he so prefer, but their vote will be only advisory, and the power to decide will still be with himself.

But let it be remembered that the exercise of these powers of the Worshipful Master cannot be so far extended as to touch the *merits of the case.* His prerogative extends to all incidental matters, but the merits must be left to the main body of the court, namely, the lodge.

It is also the right of the Worshipful Master to appoint all committees, commissioners or counsel that may be required in the course of the trial, and to preside at all meetings of said commissioners or committees. The accused may, either in person or by his counsel, object to any appointment so made, and the Worshipful Master shall decide upon the sufficiency of such objection.

The tribunal must consist solely of Master Masons; and from this rule there can be no departure.

The Master may call any Past Master temporarily to the chair during a trial, and such brother, while in the chair, may exercise all the powers of the Master; he being considered, during that time, the immediate agent of the Master.

In case of the absence, death or inability of the Worshipful Master, the Senior Warden succeeds to all his powers and duties. In case of the absence, death or inability of both the Master and Senior, the Junior Warden succeeds to the chair in like manner. The acts of either of the Wardens are in such case the acts, in legal contemplation, of the Worshipful Master; the Warden so acting *is*, for the time being, the Worshipful Master. But if the Master and both Wardens be absent, no lodge can be opened, nor any proceedings whatever taken. A Warden has no right to call a special communication of the lodge, open the same and proceed to business, while his superior officer is at home in the same village; (Decisions of G. M., No. 74.) but any action he may take in any trial or lodge proceeding by the lawful direction of his superior, will be lawful.

A Past Master cannot open the lodge and preside unless either the Worshipful Master or one of the Wardens be present; nor then without the direction or consent of the proper officer.

III.

OF THE JURISDICTION.

The penal jurisdiction of a lodge is that power which it constitutionally possesses to take judicial cognizance of Masonic offenses, and to prosecute and punish for the same. This jurisdiction is two-fold; *territorial* and *personal*. It is territorial, as existing within certain geographical limits; and personal, as attaching to certain persons, wheresoever they may be dispersed.

The territorial jurisdiction of a lodge is bounded by the geographical center between it and contiguous lodges, except in cities and villages having more than one lodge, and in case of lodges adjacent to state lines. Where there are two or more lodges in any city or village, they have concurrent jurisdiction, extending at least to the limits of such city or village (Const. of G. L., Art. 5, Sec. 5;) and in no case does the territorial jurisdiction of a lodge extend beyond the boundary of the state. A lodge has penal jurisdiction over all Masons within these limits, whether affiliated or non-affiliated, no matter of what lodge they may be members. (Const. of G. L., Art. 5, Sec. 13.)

The personal jurisdiction of a lodge extends to every one of its own members, wheresoever he may be upon the face of the globe. The allegiance of a Mason to his own lodge is indefeasible; and so long as his membership continues, he is amenable to its laws and subject to its power. Thus a Mason who resides beyond the jurisdiction of his own lodge is subject to two concurrent jurisdictions, namely, the territorial jurisdiction of the lodge where he resides, and the personal jurisdiction of his own lodge. But trial, conviction and punishment under either of these jurisdictions would exempt him from the like proceedings under the other; upon the principle that a Mason cannot be twice punished for the same Masonic offense.

But there is one person who is absolutely exempt from the penal jurisdiction of his lodge. That person is the Worshipful Master. He cannot be tried by his lodge. His lodge cannot resist his orders nor question his authority in its own body. Its only redress is by preferring charges against him in the Grand Lodge. To that supreme body, and to that alone, (or to the Grand Master in the *interim*) he is responsible for his acts while in office. Not only is he exempt from discipline in his own lodge while in office, but his lodge cannot, after his retirement from office, try or punish him for any act committed by him while in office. The Grand Lodge holds perpetual jurisdiction over his official term.

The Grand Master, while in office, is also in like manner exempt from the penal jurisdiction of the subordinate lodge of which he is a member.

Every lodge has exclusive jurisdiction in all cases of violation of its own by-laws and regulations. This is a portion of its own personal jurisdiction, which never becomes concurrent with that territorial jurisdiction which a foreign lodge acquires by the residence of a Mason within its limits.

Although our Grand Lodge has recommended (1857) that in cases where the jurisdiction is territorial merely, the subject be referred to the lodge of which the offending brother is a member, yet such reference is merely a matter of courtesy, and may be made or not, as circumstances shall require. But notice should always be given to such lodge of any proceedings actually taken.

A lodge has the same jurisdiction over Entered Apprentices and Fellow Crafts that it has over Master Masons. Every lodge of Master Masons has authority over all the degrees which it has power to confer; and as it makes Entered Apprentices and Fellow Crafts, it may, upon sufficient cause, try and expel them.

Masonry takes no judicial cognizance of the acts or offenses of a candidate committed before his initiation. If, after his initiation, he demeans himself worthily and honorably, Masonic charity veils the past, and rejoicingly aids in his reformation. (Decisions of G. M., No. 23.)

A Mason under sentence of suspension is still subject to the penal jurisdiction of the lodge. For a repetition of the offense for which he was suspended, or for any other unmasonic conduct, he may be tried, and (if the offense justify it) expelled from all the rights and benefits of Masonry, by the lodge having jurisdiction over him.

Sojourners, whether affiliated or not, are subject to penal jurisdiction in like manner as other Masons.

There are but three ways by which a Mason can be placed beyond the reach of Masonic discipline; namely, by death, by insanity (which is mental death) and by expulsion.

Where a trial is likely to result in expulsion, it should be prosecuted in the lodge in preference to the higher bodies, for the reason that a sentence of expulsion in the lodge has the effect of expelling the culprit from the lodge itself, and also from all the degrees and bodies of Masonry above the lodge; whereas the same sentence, if passed by a higher body, would not affect his standing in the lodge, but only in the body where it was passed, and those above.

The punishment of a Mason for crime by a court of law, will not bar a Masonic prosecution for the same crime. The two jurisdictions are strangers to each other. The legal tribunal, as has been intimated, inflicts a legal punishment for the *public* offense; the

Masonic tribunal inflicts a Masonic punishment for the *Masonic* offense.

It is a fixed principle of Masonic law that there is no Masonic wrong without a Masonic remedy. That remedy consists in prosecution and punishment for the wrong committed. The first step in the prosecution is the preferring of charges, which will be next considered.

IV.

OF THE CHARGES.

The preliminary questions as to the Offense, the Tribunal and the Jurisdiction having been settled, the *Charges* are next to be considered, and will demand our careful and somewhat protracted attention.

The charges (or every portion thereof proper to be written) must always be made in writing, signed by the accuser, filed with the Secretary of the lodge, and read by that officer at the next regular communication after such filing.

The offense must be charged with clearness and certainty, and time, place, persons and particulars must be distinctly specified; for every defendant is entitled to know with definiteness the nature and substance of the accusation against him, in order that he may prepare for his defense.

A general charge of unmasonic conduct, without specifications, ought not to be entertained by the Worshipful Master. Pencil writing, if clear and distinct, *may* be admissible, but as a general rule in matters of such Masonic importance it should be excluded. A loose, vague and general charge ought not to be received even in writing. If the case appears one of probability, the Master may direct that proper charges be preferred. (Decisions of G. M., No. 26.)

Mere oral charges can never be received in any case. Every particular of the offense proper to be written must be embodied, filed and read in due form, and upon the appearance of the accused those portions improper to be written must be fully stated and explained to him in open lodge, in order that he, as well as the lodge, may be particularly informed as to the whole matter.

After the charges have been read as aforesaid by the Secretary they become the property of the lodge, and they cannot thereafter be amended either in word or spirit except upon consent in open lodge, and with the full knowledge and consent of the accused. It is far better, if the charges be materially defective, to begin the prosecution *de novo*, by the filing of new Charges, than to exercise any doubtful powers of amendment. True, the ruling of the Worshipful Master, however erroneous, is law for the time being; but in case of review upon appeal to the Grand Lodge, a vast amount of trouble and inconvenience might result from his not being sustained.

Charges for offenses committed while the lodge is at labor, should be introduced by the Senior Warden;

those for offenses committed at any other time, by the Junior Warden; but should either of said officers neglect to introduce the charges, they may be introduced by any member of the lodge in good standing.

The charges ought to be preferred by a *member of the lodge*, whether the by-laws so require or not. Although this is not in all the states an absolute requirement, yet it is the almost universal practice, and by far the better one.

A profane cannot prefer charges against a Mason; neither can a Mason who is under sentence of suspension or expulsion, or non-affiliated. (Res. of G. L., No. 34.) The accuser must always be a Master Mason in good standing. (Decisions of G. M. No. 86.)

If facts are known to a profane, or to a Mason not qualified to prefer charges, involving an offense for which charges ought to be introduced, they may be communicated to any Mason who is qualified to prefer charges, and who, upon such information, may prepare and introduce the charges in due form; or the Worshipful Master may instruct one of his Wardens so to do.

If charges are preferred, or complaint made to the Worshipful Master, against an officer of the lodge, for unmasonic conduct, the Master may, in his discretion, suspend the accused at once from his office; and if the offense is an aggravated one, as gross intoxication or immorality, or a high crime or misdemeanor, he ought to do so. (Decisions of G. M., No. 43.)

Charges may be preferred against a Mason who is under sentence of suspension, and upon such charges he may be tried by his lodge for offenses committed subsequent to the sentence, or for a repetition of the offense for which he was suspended, and, if found guilty, expelled. It is not necessary that the delinquent be re-instated in order to enable the Lodge to take this action. (Decisions of G. M., No. 83.)

The Worshipful Master has the right, after charges are preferred in writing, and after examining them carefully, to declare them insufficient, and refuse to proceed to trial upon them. He ought not to entertain frivolous charges, or such as do not show clearly, if proven, a Masonic offense. (Decisions of G. M., No. 90.) If he is in doubt as to the sufficiency or competency of charges, it is proper for him to take the opinion of the lodge upon the subject by a vote ; but such opinion is merely advisory, and is of no legal force upon the Worshipful Master, who is alone responsible in the premises. He is acting as the presiding head of a legal tribunal. (Decisions of G. M., No. 91.)

FORM OF CHARGES.

To the Worshipful Master, Wardens and Brethren of......Lodge, No...., of Free and Accepted Masons.

Brother A. B., a Master Mason (or F. C., or E. A.) of (here state the residence, membership, affiliation, non-affiliation, or other masonic standing of the accused) is hereby charged with unmasonic conduct, in this, to-wit:

Specification 1—That the said A. B., on the...... day of......A. L. 58..., at the town (village or city) of......, in the county of......, State of......, did violently assault and strike Brother C. D.

Specification 2—That the said A. B., on the day and at the place aforesaid, did speak and use toward the said Brother C. D. the following scandalous and insulting language, to wit: (here set out the words used.)

Specification 3—That the said A. B., on the day and at the place aforesaid, did, in presence and hearing of several persons, speak and utter of and concerning the said Brother C. D., the following slanderous and malicious words, to wit: (here set out the words.)

All of which acts of the said A. B. were in violation of his duties and obligations as a Mason, and to the injury of the said C. D., as well as to the scandal and disgrace of the Masonic fraternity; wherefore it is demanded that the said A. B. be put upon trial therefor, aud dealt with according to Masonic law and usage.

Dated.........A. L., 58...

C.......... D..........Accuser.

If the charges are introduced by either of the Wardens, they should sign them in their official capacity.

All names should be written in full, if known. Specifications should be added for each separate state of facts constituting a Masonic offense, with reasonable certainty as to time, place, and other particulars.

FORM OF SPECIFICATIONS FOR DRUNKENNESS.

1. That the said A. B., on the......day of......, A. L. 58..., at......, in the county of......, State of......, was in a state of gross intoxication, from the intemperate use of spirituous and intoxicating liquors.

2. That the said A. B., on the......day of......, A. L. 58..., at......in the county of......, State of......, and for a long time previous thereto, to wit: for...... years last past, and at divers other places in the said county and State, and notwithstanding the frequent warnings and admonitions of the officers and brethren of this lodge, was addicted to the excessive use of intoxicating liquors, and to the evil habit of frequent and gross intoxication and drunkenness.

FORM OF SPECIFICATION FOR THEFT.

That the said A. B., on the......day of......, A. L. 58..., at......, in the county of......, State of......, did wilfully steal and take from Brother C. D. (or Mr. C. D.) of......, twenty dollars in money. (If the theft be of other property than money, describe the property.)

FORM OF SPECIFICATION FOR FRAUD.

That the said A. B., on the......day of......, A. L. 58..., at......, in the county of......, State of......, did wilfully cheat, wrong and defraud Brother C. D. by making to said C. D. certain false and fraudulent representations concerning a certain horse which he then and there sold to the said C. D., and which the said C. D. was by means of said false representations then and there induced to buy, and to pay therefor a large sum of money, to wit: the sum of one hundred dollars; which representations were that the said horse was sound, true and kind, when in fact the said horse was not such, as the said A. B. well knew.

Where the offense is non-payment of dues, regular charges must be preferred in the usual manner. A mistaken impression prevails in the minds of many Masons, that for non-payment of dues a brother may be suspended simply by a vote or resolution of the lodge, without the introduction of charges or any form of trial. Charges must be preferred, and due trial and conviction had, the same as for any other Masonic offense. (Res. of G. L. No. 19; Decisions of G. M. No. 52.)

FORM OF CHARGES FOR NON-PAYMENT OF DUES.

To the Worshipful Master, Wardens and Brethren of......Lodge, No..., of Free and Accepted Masons.

Brother A. B., a Master Mason, and a member of this lodge, is hereby charged with unmasonic conduct in wilfully violating Section...... of the By-Laws of this lodge, in this, to wit:

Specification—That the said A. B., being justly indebted to this lodge for his annual dues, accruing under said section, for the years......and......, and being able to pay the same, has neglected and refused, and still neglects and refuses to pay the same, or any part thereof, although payment of the same has been often demanded.

All of which is in violation of his duties and obligations as a Mason, and to the wrong and injury of this lodge; wherefore it is demanded that the said A. B. be put upon his trial therefor, and dealt with according to Masonic law and usage.

Dated.........A. L. 58....

C......... D........., Accuser.

When charges are preferred for violation of any provision of the Constitution or by-laws, the article or section violated should be specified with particularity, as well as the facts of the violation.

The charges and specifications having been filed with the Secretary, and read by him at the next regular communication thereafter, a true copy thereof is to be served upon the accused, together with a summons requiring him to appear and answer. A resolution to that effect having been duly passed, it is the duty of the Secretary to make the copy and issue the summons; which summons may be made returnable at any subsequent regular communication, as the lodge shall determine.

FORM OF SUMMONS, TO BE ACCOMPANIED WITH A COPY OF THE CHARGES AND SPECIFICATIONS.

To Brother A. B., of......

You are hereby summoned and required to appear at the regular communication of......Lodge, No..., of Free and accepted Masons, to be held at its Lodge Room at......, in the county of......State of......, on the......day of......, A. L., 58..., at......o'clock P. M., then and there to make answer to charges and specifications now on file against you in said lodge, a true copy of which charges and specifications is hereto annexed.

Dated.........A. L. 58....

By order of the Lodge,

E......... F...... .., Secretary.

Seal of the Lodge.

The summons and copy may be served by any Master Mason, but it is the common practice for the Secretary to make the service, unless there are reasons to prevent. The service must be made at least ten days previous to the day of trial (or return) mentioned in the summons, and a written certificate of such service, specifying the time and place thereof, should be filed by the person making the same.

CERTIFICATE OF SERVICE.

I, G. H., do hereby certify that on the......day of ......, A. L. 58..., at......in the county of......, State of......, I served personally (or at his last known place of residence) upon Brother A. B. a true copy of the charges and specifications filed against him in ......Lodge, No..., of Free and Accepted Masons, on the......day of......, A. L. 58..., by C. D., accuser, accompanied by the summons of said lodge, under the seal thereof, requiring him to appear and answer said charges and specifications at the regular communication of said lodge to be held on the......day of......A. L. 58...

Dated......A. L. 58...

G......... H.........

If the charges and summons are served by the Secretary, he should execute the foregoing certificate in his official capacity.

The service must be personal if the residence of the accused is known to the Secretary, or can be found upon due inquiry; but if his residence is not known, or cannot be ascertained, then the service may be at his last known place of residence. When the accused resides beyond the jurisdiction of the lodge in which the charges are filed, the service may be made by the Secretary of the lodge within whose jurisdiction the accused resides at the time; and the certificate of such Secretary, under the seal of his lodge, is legal evidence of due service.

The foregoing certificate of service can easily be varied so as to meet the case of service by a foreign Secretary, and a copy of the proper certificate should be sent to him in blank, enclosed with the charges and summons, in order that he may execute it under the seal of his lodge, and return it to be placed on file as evidence of the service made by him.

The accuser may choose any Master Mason as his counsel, to assist in the prosecution. If he does not appear, or chooses no counsel, the Worshipful Master may appoint such counsel in his discretion; which counsel must be a Master Mason in good standing.

The *status* of a Mason under charges is not affected until after sentence. He is presumed to be innocent until proven to be guilty; and he may, at all times before the passing of sentence, vote upon all matters not involved in the charges and specifications pending against him.

V.

OF THE ANSWER.

The charges having been properly introduced and served, and the accused duly summoned, it is his duty to appear and answer.

The answer should be in writing. If the accused answer orally, his answer should be reduced to writing by the Secretary, and made a part of the files in the case, so that no misunderstanding may afterwards arise as to its exact import.

Before answering as to the merits of the case, the accused may, if he have sufficient grounds, attack the proceedings incidentally. In so doing he may

1. Deny the jurisdiction, or
2. Deny the validity or regularity of the charges.

In either case his proposition should be made in writing, and should set forth clearly the grounds upon which it is based. The following forms will sufficiently illustrate this branch of the subject.

FORM OF DENIAL OF JURISDICTION.

To the Worshipful Master, Wardens and Brethren of......Lodge, No...., of Free and Accepted Masons.

In the matter of the charges and specifications introduced in said lodge on the......day of......A. L. 58..., by C. D., against A. B., comes the said A. B. in person (or by Y. Z. his counsel) and denies the jurisdiction of said lodge in the premises, for the following reasons, to wit:

1. Because the said A. B. did not, at the time of the introduction of said charges and specifications, reside within the territorial jurisdiction of said lodge; neither was he at that time a member of said lodge.

2. Because the acts alleged in said charges and specifications, if they were ever committed by the said A. B., were committed before his initiation in any lodge of Masons.

Wherefore the said A. B. requests that the said charges and specifications be dismissed, and that he be excused from answering thereto.

Dated...... A. L. 58...

A.......... B.........., Accused.

Any other facts which would defeat the jurisdiction should be alleged in like manner. Upon the filing and reading of such denial of jurisdiction, it is the privilege of the accused to introduce, and the duty of the lodge to receive, any proper proofs of the facts therein alleged; after which they should at once either sustain the jurisdiction or dismiss the case, as Masonic law and usage may require.

If the jurisdiction is sustained, or not denied, the accused may, if he think best, deny the validity or regularity of the charges and specifications.

FORM OF DENIAL OF VALIDITY OR REGULARITY OF THE CHARGES AND SPECIFICATIONS.

To the Worshipful Master, Wardens and Brethren of......Lodge, No..., of Free and Accepted Masons.

In the matter of the charges and specifications introduced in said lodge on the......day of......A. L. 58..., by C. D., against A. B., comes the said A. B. in person (or by Y. Z. his counsel) and denies the validity and regularity of said charges and specifications, for the following reasons, to wit:

1. Because the said C. D., the accuser, by whom said charges and specifications were introduced, was not, at the time of introducing the same, a Master Mason, (or was not a Master Mason in good standing, he being then under sentence of suspension [or expulsion] for unmasonic conduct.)

2. Because the acts alleged in the said charges and specifications are of a purely sectarian (or political) character, and do not in themselves constitute a Masonic offense.

3. Because the time (or place, or both) of the commission of the acts alleged is not set forth in said charges and specifications with reasonable distinctness.

Wherefore the said A. B. requests that the said charges and specifications be dismissed, and that he be excused from answering thereto.

Dated......A. L. 58...

A......... B........., Accused.

Under the latter, as under the former denial, the accused may make proof of any matters of fact therein alleged.

If the jurisdiction, and the validity and regularity of the charges and specifications are sustained, or not denied, the accused must then answer as to the merits ; and in so doing he may put in either one of four different answers.

1. He may answer "*guilty*," which is an unqualified admission of the entire accusation.

2. He may answer "*not guilty*," which is an unqualified denial of the entire accusation.

3. He may answer "*guilty*" as to a part, and "*not guilty*" as to another part.

4. He may admit the facts charged, and set up certain other facts or circumstances in justification or extenuation of his acts.

ANSWER OF "NOT GUILTY."

To the Worshipful Master, Wardens and Brethren of......Lodge, No..., of Free and Accepted Masons.

In the matter of the charges and specifications introduced in said lodge on the......day of......, A. L., 58..., by C. D. against A. B., comes the said A. B. in person (or by Y. Z. his counsel) and says that he is not guilty of the said charges and specifications, nor of any of them.

Dated......A. L. 58...

A......... B........., Accused.

The answer of "*guilty*" is similar to the above, simply substituting the word *guilty* for *not guilty*, and omitting the words "nor of any of them."

ANSWER OF "GUILTY" AS TO A PART, AND "NOT GUILTY" AS TO ANOTHER PART.

To the Worshipful Master, Wardens and Brethren of......Lodge, No..., of Free and Accepted Masons.

In the matter of the charges and specifications introduced in said lodge on the......day of......, A. L. 58..., by C. D. against A. B., comes the said A. B. in person (or by Y. Z. his counsel) and answers as follows, namely:

As to specification first, he says that he is guilty.

As to specification second, he says that he is not guilty.

As to specification third, he says that he is not guilty.

Dated......A. L. 58...

A......... B........., Accused.

The next following form of answer has been framed in direct response to the form of charges laid down on page 33 of this work, in order thus to afford the most practical illustration possible of the principles involved. It should therefore be read in connection with those charges.

ANSWER ADMITTING THE FACTS CHARGED, AND SETTING UP OTHER FACTS IN JUSTIFICATION AND EXTENUATION.

To the Worshipful Master, Wardens and Brethren of......Lodge, No..., of Free and Accepted Masons.

In the matter of the charges and specifications introduced in said lodge on the......day of......, A. L. 58..., by C. D. against A. B., comes the said A. B. in person (or by Y. Z. his counsel) and answers as follows, namely:

As to specification first, he admits that he did assault and strike the said C. D.; but he alleges that he did the same in necessary defense of his own person, (family or property) the said C. D. having then and there first assaulted him; and he further alleges that he used no more force than was necessary to repel the injury which the said C. D. then and there attempted against him. (Here insert any other material facts in justification.)

As to specification second, he admits that he did use toward the said C. D. the words therein specified; but he alleges that he was greatly provoked thereto by violent and abusive language then and there used toward him by the said C. D., which language was as follows: (here set forth the language, and any other material facts in extenuation.)

As to specification third, he says that he is not guilty.

Dated......A. L. 58...

A......... B....... ., Accused.

The accused may choose any Master Mason to act as his counsel, and to assist him in his defense. If the Worshipful Master has appointed, or the accuser has chosen, counsel for the prosecution, the accused may, for any good cause, object to such counsel; and *vice versa*. The Worshipful Master should thereupon, if he deems such objection well taken, remove the counsel thus objected to, and appoint, or allow to be chosen, other counsel in his stead.

All counsel in Masonic trials, whether for the prosecution or defense, must always be of the degree of Master Mason, and in good standing. (Decisions of G. M., No. 86.)

If the accused do not appear in person nor by counsel, the Worshipful Master may appoint counsel for the defense in his discretion, whose duty it will be to see that the trial is fairly conducted, and the rights of the accused not imperilled. A Mason under suspension cannot be admitted into the lodge; he *must*, therefore, appear and answer (if at all) by agent or attorney. (Decisions of G. M., No. 85.)

VI.

OF THE PROOFS.

If the charges are denied by the accused, proofs must be taken as to the facts involved.

By the affirmation of the charges and specifications on one side, and their denial on the other, an issue is raised; and that issue can only be decided upon evidence.

The proofs may be taken before the lodge, or before commissioners appointed for that purpose. If the latter course be pursued, the Worshipful Master appoints the commissioners (usually three in number) before whom, or a majority of them, all the proofs in the case should be taken. Each of the commissioners, unless present at the time of his appointment, should be immediately notified of the same by the Secretary.

NOTICE TO COMMISSIONERS.

To Brothers G. H., I. J., and K. L., of......Lodge, No..., of Free and Accepted Masons.

Please take notice, that at a regular communication of said lodge, held on the......day of......, A. L. 58..., you, and each and every of you, were appointed commissioners to take proofs in the matter of certain charges introduced in said lodge on the......day of ......, A. L. 58..., by Brother C. D. against Brother A. B.; and you, or a majority of you, are hereby directed to proceed to take all the proofs pertaining to said matter, and report the same in writing, with your doings, to said lodge, with all convenient speed.

By order of the lodge.

Dated......, A. L., 58...

E......... F........., Secretary.

{ Seal of the Lodge. }

The accused may object to either or all of the commissioners, and the Worshipful Master must decide upon the sufficiency of the objection. The commissioners should appoint a time and place of meeting for the purpose of taking testimony, of which the accuser and accused, or their counsel, must have due and reasonable (usually five days) notice. At all such meetings of commissioners the Worshipful Master has the right, *ex officio*, to be present and to preside.

In all cases the whole of the testimony, of a nature proper to be written, must be reduced to writing, and carefully preserved in the archives of the lodge.

If there be material testimony of such a nature that it cannot be produced at the place where the lodge is located, or the meetings of the commissioners held, the same may be taken by either party at any other reasonable time and place, upon permission of the Worshipful Master; due notice being first given to the opposite party, and to the Master or Secretary of the lodge.

Both the accuser and the accused, with their counsel, have the right to be present at the taking of all testimony.

NOTICE TO PARTIES TO ATTEND BEFORE COMMISSIONERS.

To Brother C. D., accuser, and Brother A. B., accused, (or their counsel, as the case may be.)

Take notice that the undersigned commissioners will meet at the hall of......Lodge, No..., of Free and Accepted Masons, at......, on the......day of......, A. L. 58..., at......o'clock in the ......noon, for the purpose of taking proofs relating to the charges preferred by Brother C. D. against Brother A. B., now pending in said Lodge; at which time and place your attendance is requested.

Dated......A. L. 58...

G......... H.........,
I.... .... J........., Commissioners.
K......... L.........,

The testimony for the prosecution must first be taken, and after the accuser shall have closed his proofs the accused may introduce the proofs for his defense. If any new matter be brought out or any new questions raised by the testimony for the defense, the prosecution may rebut the same, but cannot enter into any new matters, unless the accused be allowed to reply to the same by counter proofs.

The official books and records of the lodge are evidence in themselves; so also are the charter, constitution and by-laws of the lodge.

But the certificate of the Worshipful Master or Secretary, in the absence of entry upon the approved records of the lodge, is not sufficient evidence of the transactions of the lodge. A lodge is bound by the records which it has duly approved, and no further. It has power to amend its records, upon such evidence as is deemed sufficient; and such amended record, duly attested, has all the force and effect of an original record. But neither the Grand Lodge nor sister lodges are warranted in receiving as evidence to control their action, statements or allegations from any source, presuming the inaccuracy of said records; unless, indeed, the lodge be put upon trial before the Grand Lodge for falsifying its records, which brings up quite another matter. (Decisions of G. M., No. 25.)

The best evidence of which the circumstances of the case admit must always be produced, if possible. If the production of the best evidence be shown to be impracticable, then secondary evidence may be offered.

A witness cannot be compelled to criminate himself.

All testimony that is relevant to the facts in issue should be admitted. That which is irrelevant should be excluded. As a general rule, hearsay evidence should be excluded. Although many of those technical rules of evidence which apply in courts of law are not recognized in Masonic tribunals, yet there are certain fundamental principles of proof which must apply to all human investigation, without which rights cannot be protected and truth elicited, and among them are the few above mentioned.

Both parties have the right of cross-examination. Either party may object to any proofs offered by the other, and the Worshipful Master must decide the sufficiency of such objection. If the proofs are before commissioners, and the Worshipful Master be absent, then the commissioners may decide as to the admissibility of proofs, as the representatives, for the time being, of the Master; but if the Master be present he has power to decide.

Any discreet person is a competent witness. The testimony of a Mason may be taken upon his Masonic honor; for Masonry regards no obligation to speak the truth more binding than its own. The testimony of profanes must be upon oath, duly administered by any officer competent under the law to administer oaths. If the testimony of a profane is to be taken before the lodge, then the lodge must be called from labor to refreshment, and sit as a committee, during his introduction and examination.

The testimony of an Entered Apprentice or a Fellow Craft, if taken in open lodge, must be upon the degree corresponding to the rank of the witness; after which the lodge should be closed upon the inferior degree, and opened upon the degree of Master Mason.

During the taking of testimony before the lodge, either the Worshipful Master or any member of the lodge may put such questions as he pleases to any witness; but in case of a question being put by any member of the lodge, either party to the trial may object to such question, and the Worshipful Master shall decide upon the objection, either admitting or excluding the testimony as he may think proper; but no objection can be interposed to any question put by the Master.

A person under sentence of expulsion from all the rights and benefits of Masonry cannot testify upon his Masonic honor, for he has none. He has no part nor lot in *any* of the privileges of the Order.

The attendance of witnesses who are Masons is enforced by summons. Wilful disobedience of such summons, or a refusal to testify while under examination as a witness, is a Masonic offense, which subjects the offender to discipline.

SUMMONS FOR WITNESS TO TESTIFY BEFORE THE LODGE.

To Brother M. N.

You are hereby summoned and required to attend as a witness, at the hall of......Lodge, No..., of Free and Accepted Masons, at......, on the......day of......, A. L. 58..., at......o'clock in the......noon, then and there to testify what you may know in the matter of the charges now pending before said lodge against Brother A. B.

Dated......A. L. 58...

O......... P........., W. Master.

SUMMONS FOR WITNESS TO TESTIFY BEFORE COMMISSIONERS.

To Brother M. N.

You are hereby summoned and required to attend as a witness before Brothers......, commissioners by me appointed, at the hall of......Lodge, No..., of Free and Accepted Masons, at......, on the......day of......, A. L. 58..., at......o'clock in the......noon, then and there to testify what you may know in the matter of the charges now pending before said lodge against Brother A. B.

Dated......A. L. 58...

O......... P........., W. Master.

All summonses are to be issued by the Worshipful Master, upon application to him by either party, or his counsel.

If the witness will attend without summons, none need be issued; and no summons should in any case be issued to a profane, as he is not in any manner subject to Masonic jurisdiction.

The Secretary should carefully and particularly record all the proceedings taken in the trial. The testimony need not be entered at large upon the record, but must always be carefully preserved by the Secretary.

If the proofs are taken before commissioners, they should keep full minutes of all their proceedings, and report them, together with all the evidence, to the lodge.

It is not proper for the commissioners to report their opinion as to the guilt or innocence of the accused; they ought simply to report their doings, with the testimony taken by them, for the action of the lodge. (Rep. of Com. on Masonic Law, in G. L., 1869.)

REPORT OF COMMISSIONERS.

To the Worshipful Master, Wardens and Brethren of......Lodge, No..., of Free and Accepted Masons.

The undersigned commissioners, heretofore appointed to take proofs in the matter of the charges and specifications introduced in said lodge on the ......day of......, A. L. 58..., by Brother C. D., against Brother A. B., have discharged that duty, and beg leave to report as follows:

After five days written notice to the parties (or their counsel) the commissioners met at......, on the ......day of......A. L. 58..., at......o'clock in the ......noon. Present, Brothers G. H., I. J. and K. L., commissioners, the Worshipful Master being also present and presiding. Brother......was chosen clerk of the commission.

The accuser appeared in person, without counsel. The accused appeared in person, with......as his counsel.

The charges and specifications and the answer were then read.

Brother......was then introduced as a witness in support of the charges. The accused, by his counsel, objected to said witness being allowed to testify upon his honor as a Mason, for the reason that he was under sentence of expulsion. The fact of expulsion being made to appear, the Worshipful Master sustained the objection, and the witness was then sworn by Brother......, a Notary Public, and testified as follows:

I am a Master Mason, not in good standing. (Here insert the language of the witness in full.)

The witness was then cross-examined by the counsel for the accused, and testified as follows: (Insert his language.) The accuser then announced that he had no further proofs.

The commissioners then adjourned to meet at the same place on the......day of......, A. L. 58..., at.... o'clock in the......noon.

(Date.)

Commissioners met pursuant to adjournment. Present, Brothers G. H., I. J. and K. L., commissioners. The Worshipful Master not being present, Brother G. H. acted as chairman.

The accuser and accused appeared as before.

Brother......was then introduced as a witness for the accused, and testified upon his Masonic honor as follows: (Here insert the testimony in full.)

The official record of......Lodge, No..., of Free and Accepted Masons, of the date of......A. L. 58..., was then introduced and read in evidence, which record is as follows: (Here set out that portion of the record put in evidence in full.)

Both the accuser and accused then announced that they had no further proofs.

The proofs being closed, the commissioners adjourned without day.

Hereto annexed are the charges and specifications and the answer aforesaid, heretofore referred to the commissioners.

All of which is respectfully submitted.

G......... H...... ..
I......... J.........
K......... L...... .. } Commissioners.

Dated......A. L. 58...

If the accused does not appear, proof of service of notice upon him, or any other facts pertaining thereto, must be made before the commissioners, and embodied by them in their report. All objections, motions and rulings made by or before the commissioners must be set out in full in their report, in order that either party may take the benefit of an appeal, if he so desire.

If the accused answers that he is guilty of the charges and specifications, nothing remains but for the lodge to determine by ballot the degree of punishment to be inflicted, all necessity for the taking of proofs being obviated by such answer.

The accused should be allowed to make any statement or explanation he may choose before the lodge. Such statement or explanation is for the lodge to consider, and they may give it such credit, in whole or in part, as under all the circumstances they think it entitled to. But he cannot be cross-examined upon any statement he may make, without his consent; and if questions are put to him, he may answer them or not, as he pleases. He cannot be summoned nor subjected to examination as a witness in the case.

VII.

OF THE ARGUMENT.

Upon the closing of the proofs before the lodge, or the reception of the report of the commissioners, the accuser and accused have the right, either in person or by counsel, to argue the case before the lodge.

The usual order of discussion should be followed. The accuser, having the affirmative of the issue, opens the argument; the accused, having the negative, replies to the case made by the accuser, and urges all proper points in his own defense; the accuser then closes the argument by replying to the arguments of the accused; but the accuser should not be allowed, in closing, to raise any new questions or urge any new matters, unless leave be also given the accused to reply.

The Worshipful Master has the right to limit the parties in their argument to such time as he may think proper; but if he intends enforcing any limit he should give the parties notice before the opening of the argument; otherwise great inconvenience might be suffered.

The parties should be confined in the argument strictly to the subject matter; and no personal abuse, unmerited accusations, or violent and improper language of any kind should be allowed.

Either party may call the other to order in the argument, (as also may any member of the lodge) and when such call to order is made, the party speaking must stop, and remain silent until the point of order is decided by the Worshipful Master; and if the point of order is sustained, the party must proceed in his argument in accordance with such direction as the Worshipful Master shall give. For a refusal to comply with such direction, the Worshipful Master may seat the refractory party or counsel, or, if his conduct be grossly improper, may cause him to be immediately conducted from the lodge.

It should be remembered that the relation of parties and counsel in a Masonic trial is still that of *brethren*, and differs materially from that of parties and counsel in an action before a court of law. In any Masonic proceeding, of whatever nature, truth, candor and courtesy are never to be forgotten. Passion, invective, or recrimination ought never to be indulged, and when manifested from *any source*, at *any period* of the trial, should be promptly checked by the Worshipful Master; and especially should the Master be mindful of his own conduct in these particulars.

VIII.

OF THE DELIBERATION.

Upon the conclusion of the argument (or, if there be no argument, then upon the conclusion of the testimony) the accuser and accused, with their counsel, and every other person not authorized to vote upon the final decision of the case, must retire from the lodge. The doors should then be closed for deliberation, and no brother should be allowed to withdraw until after the sentence, except for urgent reasons.

It is proper, at this stage of the proceedings, for any brother to express his views of the case, and of the law and facts involved. A full and free interchange of ideas is often of the highest benefit at such a time. The members of the lodge are then acting as a bench of judges, to whom the pleadings and proofs have been finally submitted. They are deliberating upon their final judgment in the case, and each one has a right to whatever light and knowledge his brethren may possess. False notions are often thus eradicated, errors of fact corrected, or prejudices overcome; the result of which is the harmonious settlement of the collective mind of the lodge upon a just and equitable judgment.

Not only should the facts be carefully canvassed, but every principle of law connected with the case should be distinctly understood by every brother before the vote is taken. If there be doubt or misunderstanding as to a question of law, the best authorities should be at once consulted.

The Worshipful Master may, and should, for the information of the brethren, give his opinion as to the law; yet his judgment cannot control theirs. Each one must act independently, and upon his own individual judgment, guided by the best light which he can obtain. All are judges, and all are equal.

When every fact, interest and principle involved in the case shall have been deliberately canvassed, and when every brother shall have distinctly comprehended the issue in all its bearings, then, and not till then, the lodge will be prepared to vote upon the question of the guilt or innocence of the accused.

Let no one deem that we attach too great importance to this stage of the trial, for it is the very crisis of the case. No member should allow himself to become impatient, nor treat with indifference the slightest interest involved; but let him remember that it is his *brother* who is upon trial; and let him devote to the subject all that patient investigation and careful solicitude which he would wish that brother to devote, if himself and the accused were to exchange positions. Let that noble admonition which is so eloquently given in the Middle Chamber be borne in every heart, that in the decision of every trespass each one may judge with candor and reprehend with justice.

IX.

OF THE JUDGMENT.

Final judgment upon the guilt or innocence of the accused can only be passed in a Master Mason's lodge. None can be present but those lawfully qualified to vote upon the case; namely, all members of the lodge in good standing, except the accuser and accused, and their counsel.

An honorary member, who is not also an actual member, cannot vote nor be present. (Decisions of G. M. No. 49.) But the fact of an actual member having been also elected an honorary member, does not abridge his rights in any respect as an actual member. If he holds *both* relations to the lodge, he may exercise all the rights of both; if he holds but one, then he has only the rights of that one.

The simple question of the guilt or innocence of the accused is the one upon which the vote of the lodge is first to be taken.

The vote should be by ballot. In some states the vote is required to be taken *viva voce;* but the ballot is the only method by which secrecy can be secured, and it is in strict accordance with Masonic usage. A Mason has the same right to a secret ballot here as in voting upon the initiation or advancement of a candidate. He cannot be questioned, in the lodge nor elsewhere, as to how he voted. To his own conscience and to his God he is alone responsible. Where, as in some jurisdictions, every brother is required to rise and declare his vote in open lodge, the independence and freedom of individual action are in many instances greatly impaired, and the ends of justice thereby often defeated. A brother may have the strongest and most honorable reasons for concealing his vote from the accused: a thing which it would be *practically* impossible for him to do except by a secret ballot, however *theory* may run to the contrary.

The vote should be taken upon each charge or specification separately; and the lodge may acquit or convict upon a part or all of the charges and specifications, as they may deem just.

The particular method of balloting lies in the discretion of the Worshipful Master; though the ball ballot is more strictly Masonic. If it be by ball ballot, the usual practice is to cast black for "guilty," and white for "not guilty"; if paper ballots are cast, the words "not guilty," or "guilty," should be plainly written, and the ballots so folded that they cannot be read as they are cast.

The Worshipful Master and Wardens are the proper officers to inspect and declare the ballot.

Two thirds of all the votes cast are required to convict.

There being no possibility of a tie where a majority of two thirds is required, the Worshipful Master has the same vote as any other member, and no more.

The result of the ballot upon each charge or specification should be recorded by the Secretary in regular order, with the numbers severally cast for "guilty" and "not guilty."

No brother can be excused from voting except by the unanimous consent of the lodge.

If it appear, upon counting the ballots, that less than two thirds are cast for "guilty," the accused stands acquitted, and the judgment of the lodge must be so recorded and declared forthwith.

Upon a judgment of acquittal, the proceedings are absolutely terminated, and the case is closed, so far as regards any further action by the lodge. There can be no reconsideration of the vote, nor repassing of the ballot. The only remedy is by appeal to the Grand Lodge.

But if the accused be convicted upon any or all of the charges and specifications, the question immediately arises as to the penalty that shall be inflicted.

To the consideration of Masonic penalties, their nature and consequences, the attention of the reader will be directed in the next chapter.

X.

OF THE PENALTY.

The accused having been found guilty, in the manner set forth in the preceding chapter, it only remains for the lodge to inflict such lawful penalty as, under all the circumstances, shall be deemed most just.

But three penalties are known to Masonic jurisprudence, viz:

1. Expulsion.
2. Suspension (either definite or indefinite.)
3. Reprimand.

The first is an absolute dissolution of all Masonic ties; an utter destruction of all Masonic rights. It is Masonic death.

The second is a temporary deprivation of the privileges of the Order, for a period during which the Masonic rights of the offender are held in abeyance, or suspense, but are not entirely destroyed.

The third is a mere expression of censure or disapprobation, without any deprivation, either temporary or otherwise, of Masonic rights and privileges.

Expulsion is the severest punishment Masonry inflicts. Not only does it rupture all the ties which bind the delinquent to the fraternity, but the result of his iniquity is visited upon the heads of his wife and children; and both he and they are from thenceforth as much strangers to the Order as though he had never been a Mason. Neither he nor they are entitled to any Masonic relief whatever. He is no longer subject to the penal jurisdiction of the lodge. He cannot visit any lodge, nor be recognized fraternally by any individual Mason, nor join in any Masonic procession or ceremony, nor prefer charges in any lodge, nor testify as a Mason upon any Masonic trial, nor receive the honors of Masonic burial.

Expulsion from the lodge expels, without further action, from all other Masonic bodies with which the accused may be connected—whether a chapter of Royal Arch Masons, a council of Royal and Select Masters, or a commandery of Knights Templar. But expulsion from any superior body—as from a chapter, council, or commandery—does not expel from the lodge, nor from any degree or body in Masonry below the one in which the sentence is passed. The three degrees which every lodge confers are the foundation upon which Freemasonry, in *all* its degrees and departments, rests. When this foundation is removed, the entire Masonic edifice must fall. But the removal of any portion of the superstructure does not, for evident reasons, affect that which lies beneath. A further and most conclusive reason for this rule is also found in the obligation of the third degree.

The penalty of expulsion being of so severe a nature, it should only be inflicted after the clearest proof, and for the greatest offenses. Yet in cases which render it necessary, it should be promptly and firmly administered. No false ideas of mercy should be allowed to overbear the well-being and safety of the whole society, for these are to be maintained at every hazard; "that the honor, glory and reputation of the institution may be firmly established, and the world at large convinced of its good effects." The cause of justice, the dignity and authority of the law, and the fair fame of the Order, are matters of far greater moment than any personal interests of the offender.

It is the theory of the law in this country, as well as in England, that the subordinate lodge has power to try the delinquent, and upon conviction, to pronounce the sentence of expulsion, but that the sentence must be confirmed by the Grand Lodge, to make it final. This confirmation is given (except in case of appeal) by the silent reception of the report of the Secretary of the subordinate lodge; and, by Masonic usage, the sentence of the lodge stands in full force in *all cases*, until formally revoked by the Grand Lodge. (Decisions of G. M., No. 20.)

Suspension, whether definite or indefinite, subjects the offender, for the time being, to nearly the same disabilities as expulsion, except that those disabilities are temporary instead of permanent. During the period of his actual suspension, he is prohibited from the exercise and enjoyment of any of his Masonic privileges. His rights are placed in abeyance—or, as the sentence implies, *suspension*—and he can neither visit or join other lodges, nor hold Masonic communication, nor receive fraternal relief or fellowship from any Masonic body or brother whomsoever, during the period of his suspension. But he is still a Mason. He is still subject to the penal jurisdiction of the lodge. His Masonic relations are not lost nor destroyed, but only temporarily interrupted; to be resumed in their fullness as soon as the period of his suspension shall expire, or his sentence be revoked.

Definite and indefinite suspensions are precisely similar in their immediate effects, and differ only as regards the time of their continuance and the manner of restoration from their disabilities.

Definite suspension ceases upon the expiration of the period for which it was declared, being terminated by mere lapse of time.

Indefinite suspension continues, as the term indicates, *indefinitely;* that is, until the lodge interposes by its act of restoration; being terminated, not by lapse of time, but by the positive action of the tribunal by whose sentence it was inflicted.

A singular conflict of authority exists among the

various jurisdictions of the United States upon the question of definite and indefinite suspension. While some Grand Lodges hold that definite suspension is illegal, and that indefinite suspension alone is legal, others hold with equal tenacity to the exact contrary, declaring that indefinite suspension is illegal, and that definite suspension alone is legal. Amidst all this confusion I find by far the greater weight of opinion, as well as of usage, sustaining the legality of *both* of these penalties, and upholding the right of lodges to inflict either of them, in their discretion; ranking indefinite suspension as the severer penalty of the two, and consequently first in order upon the ballot.

The consideration of the second point of distinction between definite and indefinite suspension, namely, the several methods of restoration from their disabilities, will be deferred until a subsequent chapter.

A delinquent under sentence of suspension, whether definite or indefinite, (or of expulsion) is not liable to pay dues. Lodge dues are paid for the enjoyment of certain rights which pertain to membership, and payment for the privileges of membership is suspended upon the suspension or cessation of that membership. It would certainly be against all principles of equity to compel payment of dues, while the very consideration of those dues was withheld.

Reprimand is the mildest form of Masonic punishment, and consists in a formal reproof, administered by the Worshipful Master in open lodge, in pursuance of a sentence of the lodge to that effect. It does not in any way affect the Masonic standing of the accused. It deprives him of no privileges, and abridges none of his rights.

The terms to be used in the infliction of this penalty are of course left to the discretion of the Worshipful Master, but he should remember that the punishment consists in the fact that the reprimand has been ordered, and not in any particular severity of language, and should therefore avoid any uncourteous remarks. No mere words can add anything to the ignominy of the sentence.

The distinction which some writers endeavor to make between public and private reprimand, and between reprimand and censure, is not warranted by Masonic law nor sanctioned by any correct usage. It but serves as an illustration of those distinctions without difference, the only tendency of which is to darken the subject which they are designed to elucidate.

It is an inflexible principle of Masonic law that no Mason can be suspended nor expelled, nor in any way punished, nor deprived of any Masonic right or privilege whatsoever, without charges and specifications regularly filed, and due trial and lawful conviction thereupon, with opportunity to the accused to appear and defend. (Res. of G. L., No. 19.) This principle has been affirmed with one unanimous voice by Grand Lodges and leading Masonic jurists throughout the world; and yet there is an opinion in the minds of thousands of Masons that for non-payment of dues, and some other delinquencies, the name of the delinquent may be stricken from the roll, and his membership thereby temporarily suspended, by a mere resolution of the lodge, without any charges, notice or trial whatever; and the erroneous practice actually prevails in many lodges.

The so-called penalty of "*striking from the roll,*" or "*exclusion,*" is in direct violation of Masonic law, unknown to correct Masonic usage, and should not be considered for an instant within the walls of any well regulated lodge. The Worshipful Master has the power, by his prerogative, to exclude *any one* from the lodge, upon such reasons as may seem to him sufficient; but it is a power incident only to *his* office. It is not in the nature of a penalty, but a protection; and with the exercise of that power the lodge neither has nor can have anything whatever to do, either by its by-laws or by any judicial action.

Neither can membership be suspended or terminated, nor any other deprivation or penalty inflicted by the mere operation of a by-law, without opportunity to defend or explain; and any by-law to that effect is absolutely void, as being in conflict with the constitution of Masonry. *No penalty whatever* can be inflicted except after due trial and lawful conviction.

The infliction of fines as a penalty upon refractory members or brethren is also inconsistent with ancient Masonic law and usage. (Res. of G. L., No. 15.)

After the ballot by which the accused is convicted, the vote must be taken upon the penalty in the following order, beginning with the highest and descending to the lowest, until the requisite vote is given to declare the sentence; viz:

1. Expulsion.
2. Indefinite Suspension.
3. Definite Suspension.
4. Reprimand.

The vote should be by ballot, and the same rules regulate the ballot here as in passing judgment upon the question of guilt or innocence.

A two thirds vote is required for sentence of expulsion or suspension. (Const. of G. L., Art. 6, Sec. 4.)

Sentence of reprimand may be passed by a majority vote.

The severity of the penalty is not regulated in the Masonic, as in the municipal law, by the particular offense committed, but rests solely in the discretion of the lodge having jurisdiction in the case. Any one (but *only* one) of the three Masonic penalties may be inflicted for any Masonic offense, unless there be special provisions of law to the contrary; all the facts and circumstances being taken into consideration by the lodge in fixing the sentence. But when special constitutional or legal provisions are laid down (Const. of G. L., Art. 6, Sec. 13.) those provisions must of course be followed; and if, as is the case in some lodges, the by-laws provide a particular one of the three Masonic penalties for a particular offense (as for instance, that the penalty for non-payment of dues shall be limited to suspension) the lodge must be governed by the limitation so provided. But if the by-laws provide a penalty or proceeding unknown to Masonry; as, for example, a fine, or striking from the roll, or exclusion from the lodge, or forfeiture of office; such provision is null and void, and should be so treated, for though every lodge has the power to regulate its internal police by the adoption of by-laws, yet such by-laws must be consistent both with the Constitution of the Grand Lodge and with the ancient landmarks and usages of Masonry. (Const. of G. L., Art. 6, Sec. 6.)

If the case shall seem to warrant such a course, the lodge may refrain from inflicting any penalty whatever; in which event the Masonic standing of the accused will not in any way be affected. Although the judgment of conviction will still stand against him, yet his legal relations to the Order will remain unchanged; for the loss of Masonic rights is the result of the *sentence*, and not of the *conviction*. It is the *penalty* of expulsion or suspension, and not the *judgment* of "guilty," that changes the *status* of the delinquent.

If, in voting upon all the Masonic penalties in their proper order, there shall not be obtained the requisite vote for the infliction of any penalty whatever, the lodge cannot reconsider its action and inflict punishment by a subsequent vote.

The result of the vote upon each penalty should

be entered at large upon the record, with the number of votes *pro* and *con* in each instance, and in the order in which the proceedings occur.

After the lodge has completed its action, the accuser and accused, with their counsel, should be re-admitted, and the result announced to them by the Worshipful Master.

If not present, they should at once be officially notified of the action of the lodge by the Secretary.

NOTICE OF JUDGMENT AND SENTENCE.

To Brothers A. B. and C. D. (or to either of the parties or their counsel, as the case may be.)

Take notice that in the matter of the charges and specifications introduced in......Lodge, No..., of Free and Accepted Masons on the......day of......A. L. 58..., by Brother C. D. against Brother A. B., the said lodge did on the......day of......, A. L. 58..., adjudge the said A. B. guilty of said charges, and of specifications Nos. 1 and 2 made thereunder; but of specification No. 3 it did adjudge him not guilty; and thereupon the said lodge did pass sentence of...... (state the penalty particularly) against the said A. B., which sentence now stands recorded against him in said lodge.

Dated......A. L. 58...

E......... F........., Secretary.

If no sentence was passed, let the notice so specify.

All cases of expulsion, except for non-payment of dues, are required to be reported forthwith to the R. W. Grand Secretary of the Grand Lodge. (Const. of G. L., Art. 6, Sec. 8.) If the person expelled or suspended were a member of another lodge than the one wherein he was tried, the lodge in which he held his membership should be immediately notified of the proceedings.

Here the case closes, unless an appeal be taken.

XI.

OF APPEALS.

Any brother deeming himself aggrieved by the decision of his lodge, or of the Master thereof, may appeal, in writing, to the Grand Lodge. (Ancient Landmarks, No. 13; Const. of G. L., Art. 6, Sec. 5.)

This great right is inalienable and indefeasible; and it is not in the power of any Grand Lodge, nor of any body of Masons whomsoever, to deny, abridge, repeal or modify it. It extends as well to Fellow Crafts and Entered Apprentices as to Master Masons; it includes within its protection the rights of the humblest and the weakest, as well as of the highest and the strongest. Whosoever is subject to Masonic jurisdiction, is entitled to his redress by appeal to the tribunal of last resort.

The features of a Masonic appeal are that it may be taken by either party, and without regard to whether the accused were acquitted or convicted upon the trial. It applies as well in questions of law as in questions of fact, and lies from any erroneous action, ruling or decision, whether of the lodge, of the Worshipful Master, or of commissioners. It is, in short, the method, and the only method, whereby any error whatsoever (except as hereinafter mentioned) may be taken from the lodge to the Grand Lodge for review and correction.

The appeal must be taken, and notice thereof given in writing to the subordinate lodge by filing the same with the Secretary thereof, within ninety days after the appellant shall have received official notice of the decision from which the appeal is taken; otherwise the appeal will not be entertained by the Grand Lodge. (Res. of G. L., No. 17.)

NOTICE OF APPEAL.

To......Lodge, No..., of Free and Accepted Masons.

Take notice that I intend to appeal from the action (or decision) of said lodge (or of the Worshipful Master of said lodge, or of the commissioners appointed to take proofs, or all of them,) in the matter of the charges preferred against me by Brother C. D., whereby I was convicted of said charges, and sentence of......passed against me; (or set forth any other decision from which appeal is taken) and you are hereby requested to make out and forward to the Grand Secretary of the Grand Lodge of Free and Accepted Masons of the State of Michigan certified copies of all papers, proofs, records and proceedings pertaining to said matter, preparatory to the trial of said appeal at the next annual communication of the said Grand Lodge.

Dated......A. L. 58...

A......... B...... ..

If the appeal be taken from the action or decision of the Worshipful Master in a matter disconnected from any trial, the notice should specify the subject matter fully; otherwise following the same general form as above, and varying it in accordance with the facts.

Upon the receipt of this notice it is the duty of the Secretary to immediately make and transmit to the Grand Secretary full and accurate copies, duly certified, of the proceedings in the case as they are recorded upon the books of the lodge, of the charges and specifications, answer or answers, notices, summonses, proofs, reports, and all matters in the archives of the lodge pertaining to the subject matter: in order that the Grand Lodge may be enabled to come to a proper understanding and speedy decision thereof.

The Secretary should minute the notice and return upon the records of the lodge, in order that the history of the case may be clear in case papers should be lost.

The appeal must be made in writing, and should set forth the grounds upon which the appellant seeks redress.

FORM OF APPEAL.

To the M. W. Grand Lodge of Free and Accepted Masons of the State of Michigan.

The undersigned hereby appeals to you from the decision of......Lodge, No..., of Free and Accepted Masons, in the matter of certain charges and specifications preferred in said lodge against this appellant by C. D., whereby this appellant was convicted of the said charges and specifications, and sentence of suspension passed against him; and he specifies the following as the ground of his appeal, viz:

1. That the charges and specifications are vague, uncertain and insufficient.

2. That the commissioners erred in refusing to admit the sworn affidavit of J. K.

3. That the Worshipful Master erred in allowing O. S. to act as counsel for the accuser, the said O. S. being at the time under sentence of suspension.

4. That the proofs were not sufficient to warrant the conviction.

5. That the severity of the penalty is disproportionate to the offense proven.

6. That the lodge erred in passing sentence of suspension by a majority vote.

7. That judgment and sentence were passed while the lodge was open upon the second degree of Masonry.

All of which will more fully appear from the records, proofs and proceedings in the case.

Dated......A. L. 58...

A......... B........., Appellant.

Any other matters upon which the appeal is grounded should be set forth in like manner, care being taken to specify them definitely and in order.

The appeal may be taken generally, upon all matters involved in the case; or specially, upon any decision or decisions, irregularity or irregularities, occurring in the course of the proceedings.

The appeal should be filed with the Grand Secretary, which filing completes the steps to be taken by the appellant until the Grand Lodge shall convene.

No copy or notice of the appeal is required to be served upon the appellee. The notice to the lodge becomes, when filed, a part of the record in the case, of which the appellee is bound to take notice.

No formal answer to an appeal is necessary, although one is sometimes put in; and for the convenience of those who may desire to follow that practice, the following general form is given:

ANSWER TO APPEAL.

To the M. W. Grand Lodge of Free and Accepted Masons of the State of Michigan.

In the matter of the appeal of A. B. from the decision of......Lodge, No..., of Free and Accepted Masons.

Comes C. D., appellee (or the said Lodge, or O. P., Worshipful Master of said Lodge, as the case may be) and in answer to said appeal denies that there was any error in the proceedings of said lodge; (or of the said Worshipful Master, or of the commissioners) and further says that the same is sustained by the evidence in the case and by the law applicable thereto.

Dated......A. L. 58...

C......... D........., Appellee.

If any answer be made to the appeal it should be filed with the Grand Secretary in like manner as the appeal, but no notice thereof is required to be made upon the appellant. Any special matters that the appellee may desire to set up can be covered by amplification of the above form of answer.

It is lawful to appeal directly to the Grand Master when the Grand Lodge is not in session; but inasmuch as his decision is subject to review by the Grand Lodge, it is preferable to make the appeal to the Grand Lodge directly, where alone a *final* decision can be had. And furthermore, any interlocutory order which the appellant may desire to obtain from the Grand Master, as the stay of proceedings under the sentence, for instance, can be obtained as well upon the filing of the appeal and return with the Grand Secretary as though the appeal had been made to the Grand Master himself; for upon his attention being called to the facts and proceedings as embodied in the return or transcript sent up by the Secretary, the Grand Master may make such interlocutory order as the case shall demand; which order will be of force until reviewed by the Grand Lodge.

In case the appeal be made to the Grand Master instead of to the Grand Lodge, the notice of appeal should be framed with that view, and the appeal should be directed to him in his official character, otherwise following the general forms above laid down. The appeal and Secretary's return should in such case be remitted to the Grand Master, instead of to the Grand Lodge.

As has been remarked in a preceding chapter, no appeal can ever be taken from any action, ruling or decision of the Worshipful Master to the lodge itself. It is the prerogative of the Worshipful Master to rule and govern his lodge, answering for his conduct only to his Masonic superiors, namely, the Grand Lodge, or, in the *interim* thereof, to the Grand Master. The fact that this results in the vesting of dictatorial power in the Master within his own lodge, constitutes no real objection to the principle; for the ancient institution of Freemasonry is not based upon those principles of republican liberty and popular rights which are the only sure foundation and support of municipal governments, but upon those ideas of patriarchal supremacy which pervaded the world during the ages in which Freemasonry took its rise. Notwithstanding the undoubted necessity of political freedom as the basis of public peace and prosperity, experience has proven the despotic powers of the Master to be the very ægis of our Masonic system—its sure protection against faction and discord within, and its strong defense against invading malice from without. In the hour of peril, the only safety lies in the prompt and powerful action of a single will; and accordingly we find that in all well organized governments, whether free or despotic, the executive power is placed in a single hand. It was the judicious exercise of the supreme power of the Grand Masters that saved the craft in Europe from destruction during the terrible persecutions waged against it by the Roman Pontiff in the thirteenth century.

Yet the powers of the Worshipful Master are by no means without prudent checks and balances. His vows and obligations are of the most sacred and binding character, and that supreme appellate tribunal, the Grand Lodge, under whose watchful eye his every act must be performed, wields over him a power even more despotic than that which he exercises within the narrow limits of his own subordinate jurisdiction. His responsibility is proportionate to his power; the account which he must render is commensurate with the high charge committed to his hands.

That able Masonic writer, Dr. Mackey, observes that "some writers have endeavored to restrain the despotic authority of the Master to decisions in matters strictly relating to the work of the lodge, while they contend that on all questions of business an appeal may be taken from his decision to the lodge. But it would be unsafe, and often impracticable, to draw this distinction; and accordingly the highest Masonic authorities have rejected the theory and denied the power in a lodge to entertain an appeal from any decision of the presiding officer." In alluding to the safeguards that are thrown around this power, he further says, "the appellate court of the jurisdiction is ever ready to listen to appeals, to redress grievances, to correct the errors of an ignorant Master, and to punish the unjust decisions of an iniquitous one."

The Worshipful Master not only *may*, but *must*, sustain his own prerogative. He cannot, even by courtesy, entertain an appeal to the lodge from any decision of the chair; and to do so would be a palpable violation of a well established principle of Masonic law.

The decision of an officer lawfully occupying the chair *pro tempore* has the same force, and is governed by precisely the same rules, as though made by the Worshipful Master himself.

No appeal lies from the action of a subordinate lodge (if regularly taken) in the admission of members or the election and initiation of candidates. The choice and regulation of its own membership is an inherent right of the lodge, with which the Grand Lodge has no power to interfere. "Nor is this inherent privilege subject to a dispensation; because the members of a particular lodge are the best judges of it." (Gen. Reg. of 1721, No. 6.) For any *irregularity* in such action, as, for example, balloting upon an inferior degree, or initiation upon a ballot found not clear, an appeal may be taken; but not upon the question of the power and right of the lodge to admit or reject, for that is a portion of that original control which has always been exercised, and never delegated, by the subordinate (or "particular") lodges.

The appeal must be prosecuted at the first regular communication of the Grand Lodge after the time limited for taking the same shall have expired. (Res. of G. L., No. 17.)

Upon the trial of the appeal the Grand Lodge of course adopts such method as it deems most proper; but the usual practice is to refer the appeal, with the testimony and all matters connected therewith, to a committee, who, upon such reference, make a full investigation of the case, and report all material facts and questions involved therein, with a recommendation of the decision which, in the opinion of the committee, the merits of the case require. Upon the coming in of this report the Grand Lodge takes final action in the case, in like manner as though the investigation of the matter had been made by and before the whole body. If the report be unsatisfactory or incomplete, the case may be re-committed to the same or another committee for further examination, or such further examination may be made before the whole body of the Grand Lodge, as shall be deemed most expedient. The Grand Lodge may direct the amendment of the report of the committee in any particular, and, in its sovereign pleasure, may adopt, reject or vary any recommendation embodied therein.

A case will not be reversed upon appeal for mere matter of form, provided substantial justice shall have been done; but any error or irregularity in any paper or proceeding whereby any right shall have been withheld, any privation suffered, or any wrong or inequality caused, will be considered, and such order made in the premises as fairness and equity shall demand, whether it be of reversal, modification or new trial. A reasonable adherence to forms and precedents is necessary in every judicial proceeding, and justice between man and man can only be reached by systematic methods of inquiry and adjudication. The moment any tribunal departs from that established system of procedure which is sanctioned by law and usage, that moment the rights of all parties are endangered; for where there is no standard there is no protection. Therefore a proper adherence to those rules and forms which precedent has sanctioned should always be enforced in subordinate jurisdictions, unless rendered absolutely impracticable by the circumstances of the case. Urgent necessity can alone justify a departure from settled forms and methods, and a return to them should instantly follow the removal of that necessity.

The Grand Lodge, or, in the *interim* thereof, the Grand Master, may order the Secretary of the lodge from which the appeal is made to amend his report or transcript in whatever matter shall be deemed necessary, to the end that a complete understanding of the whole case may be had.

It is competent for the Grand Lodge to receive any new evidence upon the trial of the appeal, for it not only holds appellate jurisdiction in the case, but it is also the supreme Masonic authority, subject only to its own Constitution and the Landmarks of the Order; but no such evidence ought to be received by the Grand Lodge without reasonable notice being first given by the party desiring to take the same to the opposite party, specifying with particularity the nature of the evidence thus sought to be introduced. What is reasonable notice in such case is for the Grand Lodge to determine, and the opposite party must have full opportunity to rebut the new evidence thus introduced.

NOTICE OF INTENTION TO TAKE NEW PROOFS UPON TRIAL OF APPEAL BEFORE THE GRAND LODGE.

To......Lodge, No...., of Free and Accepted Masons.

Take notice that in the matter of the appeal from the decision of said lodge, now pending before the Grand Lodge of Free and Accepted Masons of the State of Michigan, the undersigned will, upon the trial of said appeal, at the next annual communication of said Grand Lodge, offer the following proofs, in addition to those already on file and of record. (Here state the particular matters intended to be proven.)

Dated...... A. L. 58...

A......... B........., Appellant.

In some jurisdictions a Court of Appeals is established by the Grand Lodge, by and before whom all appeals are tried. Where this practice prevails, such court has full power to try and determine all matters pertaining to cases coming properly before it, under such regulations as the Grand Lodge may adopt for its government; and the decisions and orders of such court, made within the established powers thereof, are of the same binding force and authority as though made by the Grand Lodge itself. By whatever name such a court may be called, or with whatever powers it may be invested, it is still, in legal effect nothing more than a committee of the Grand Lodge. Its action is simply the action of the Grand Lodge, by its agent or referee. Though appeals be authorized directly to such a court, they may still be taken directly to the Grand Lodge; for the right to appeal to that supreme body is a landmark of the Order, which not even the Grand Lodge can abridge or alter. The trial before a Court of Appeals is, then, only another method of *trial by the Grand Lodge;* and it is not possible for the Grand Lodge, by vesting judicial power in such a tribunal, to divest itself of its own jurisdiction and responsibility in the premises. It may *authorize,* but cannot lawfully *compel,* the taking of appeals to another bar than its own. To the Grand Lodge itself the aggrieved appellant has still the right to pray, and to his prayer the Grand Lodge is still bound to listen.

APPEAL FROM GRAND MASTER TO GRAND LODGE.

To the M. W. Grand Lodge of Free and Accepted Masons of the State of Michigan.

The undersigned hereby appeals to you from the decision of the M. W. Grand Master, made in and by his order of June 30th, A. L. 58..., in the case of the appeal of this appellant from the decision of ......Lodge, No..., to the said Grand Master, whereby the decision of said lodge was sustained.

For the grounds of this appeal reference is hereby made to the particular statement of the same as made in the appeal from said lodge to the Grand Master; consideration of which is hereby respectfully asked.

Dated......A. L. 58....

A......... B........., Appellant.

Notice of this appeal should be given to the Grand Master and served upon the subordinate lodge.

After a due investigation of the case, the Grand Lodge may, by a majority vote—

1. Affirm the decision appealed from.
2. Reverse the decision.
3. Modify or change the decision.
4. Award a new trial.

If the penalty be too severe, the Grand Lodge may inflict a milder one; if not sufficient, it may adjudge one more severe. It may sustain the judgment and revoke or alter the sentence, or it may set aside both together. It has, in short, sovereign jurisdiction in the premises, subject only to the limitations before mentioned.

If the decision of the subordinate lodge be affirmed, the Masonic standing of the accused will remain precisely as fixed by the decision of the subordinate tribunal.

If a new trial be awarded, the *status* of the accused will be, in the mean time, that of a Mason under charges.

Consideration of the effect of a reversal or modification of the decision appealed from will be deferred to the chapter upon Restoration.

XII.

OF NEW TRIALS.

If the Grand Lodge is dissatisfied with the decision made below, but is still unwilling, either from inadequacy of proof or any other reason, to make any final order in the premises, it refers the case back to the subordinate lodge for a new trial.

In the mean time (unless some further or different order be made by the Grand Lodge) the Masonic standing of the accused is that of a Mason under charges; for inasmuch as the decision of the subordinate tribunal has been reviewed by the Grand Lodge, and *not sustained*, but a new trial ordered, the lodge must retrace its steps, and the old conviction and sentence (or acquittal, if that were the decision) stand for naught. The decision is annulled, though the proceedings continue.

The new trial proceeds, unless special order be made to the contrary, upon the charges and answer already on file, and begins at the introduction of the proofs. No amendments can be made of the charges and specifications except under the like restrictions as at first, and none of the answer except upon application of the accused and permission of the Worshipful Master.

The proofs upon the new trial may be taken before the lodge or before commissioners, as the lodge shall determine, without regard to which method was formerly pursued. If they be taken before commissioners, the Worshipful Master may continue the commissioners before appointed, or appoint new ones, in his discretion; but in either case there is the same right of objection as before.

In the matter of the selection of counsel, the same rules and the same right of objection apply as in the original trial.

From the opening of the proofs, the case proceeds under precisely the same rules and regulations as though it had never before been tried.

The parties are not limited to the evidence produced at the former trial, but either of them may introduce any new proofs he may please, subject only to those general rules which govern the introduction of proofs in all Masonic trials. But the proofs must begin and proceed *de novo*. The proofs taken and recorded upon the former trial cannot be received and considered as evidence of the facts therein stated, unless both parties shall freely consent that they be so considered. In other words, proofs made upon a former trial cannot be treated as evidence in the new trial, unless they be made and introduced anew, in like manner as at first. The parties may stipulate to waive this rule of evidence, as they may any other; but if any such stipulation be made, it should be particularly minuted in the recording of the proofs.

Upon the final decision of the case, the lodge may acquit or convict the accused, or inflict any one of the Masonic penalties, or none at all, as it shall deem most just; being governed in no respect whatever by its former action.

If, on account of some fault in the charges and specifications, or for any other reason, it shall be deemed unsafe or inexpedient to proceed to a new trial, the case may be entirely abandoned, and prosecution be instituted *de novo*, by the filing of new charges and specifications. The lodge is not *obliged*, upon the case being remanded for new trial, to try it a second time. It then stands like any other case before the lodge, ready for the introduction of proofs, and may be prosecuted or abandoned, as the accuser shall desire.

If, upon new trial, the accused be a second time convicted, he may again appeal to the Grand Lodge; and no number of convictions or acquittals can exhaust the right of either party to appcal—a right inalienable and indestructible in every Mason.

In case the accuser do not proceed with the prosecution within a reasonable time after the remanding of the case for a new trial, the Worshipful Master may either appoint counsel and direct that the trial proceed, or dismiss the charges, as, in view of all the circumstances, he shall think to be proper; and the one or the other he ought most certainly to do; for the accused has the right here, as everywhere, to a speedy and impartial trial by his peers, while it is always the province of the Master to forbid a prosecution upon frivolous or insufficient charges. (Decisions of G. M., Nos. 90 and 91.) No lodge or Master has the right to subject a brother to the disgrace and mortification of charges pending against him without a prospect of immediate trial. The Worshipful Master should make it a rule to dispose of every Masonic trial with all reasonable dispatch, and in case of neglect or refusal to prosecute a case, to dismiss it from the lodge.

A brother under sentence may obtain a new trial at once, without appeal, by exhibiting satisfactory reasons therefor to the Grand Lodge or Grand Master, who may thereupon order a new trial. But the lodge can only grant a new trial by an unanimous vote. (Decisions of G. M., No. 48.) After a new trial is granted by the lodge, precisely the same rules govern it as though it were granted by the Grand Lodge. A form of petition for new trial will be found in the chapter on Grand Lodge Trials, which can readily be adapted for use in the subordinate lodge.

XIII.

OF RESTORATION.

Restoration is the reinstatement of a suspended or expelled Mason to his standing in the Order, either in whole or in part.

The effect of restoration may be the re-investment of the delinquent with the rights and benefits of Masonry merely, without membership in any lodge; or its effect may be to renew both his general rights as a Mason and his membership in a particular lodge; according as the nature of the case shall be.

Restoration follows as the result of one of three different causes, viz:

1. Act of law.
2. Act of the lodge.
3. Act of the Grand Lodge.

Restoration occurs *by act of law* in case of definite suspension only. Where sentence of suspension for a fixed and determinate period is passed against a Mason, he is, upon the termination of that period, instantly restored to all those rights and privileges from which he stood suspended; without any further action either upon his own part or upon the part of the lodge wherein the sentence was passed, but by mere operation of law. The termination of the sentence is the termination of the suspension; and the punishment being expressly limited by the tribunal inflicting it, that punishment cannot be continued, nor any deprivation of Masonic rights extended, beyond the prescribed limit. This restoration is both to the rights of Masonry and to the rights of membership; for suspension, as already remarked in the chapter upon Masonic penalties, is not a total destruction, but a temporary interruption, of Masonic rights. But restoration from definite suspension does not revive any Masonic rights which did not exist at the time the sentence took effect. It restores the delinquent to his former position, and nothing more. If he holds an office when sentence is passed upon him, the sentence suspends him from his office, as from every other Masonic franchise; and if his restoration occurs before his term of office expires, he is restored to his office as well as to every other franchise which he enjoyed at the time of passing of sentence upon him. If the office terminates before the suspension, of course there is no restoration to the office.

Restoration *by act of the lodge* may occur in case of definite suspension, of indefinite suspension, or of expulsion.

If one under sentence of definite suspension shall

by good behavior and apparent reformation seem to merit a remission of some portion of the penalty pronounced against him, the lodge may, at any time before the expiration of the period of his suspension, restore him to all his former rights by a two-thirds vote. This action may be either by the voluntary motion of the lodge, or upon petition of the brother under sentence. The effect of such restoration will be precisely the same as though the period of his sentence had elapsed, and he had been restored by operation of law.

The lodge may restore from indefinite suspension in the same manner and for the same causes as in case of definite suspension, and with the like effect: the only difference between the two cases being, that where sentence of indefinite suspension is passed, no restoration can ever take place except by positive action of the lodge or of the Grand Lodge; whereas restoration follows a sentence of definite suspension inevitably, and by force of law, upon the lapse of the sentence, but *may* take place by act of the lodge or of the Grand Lodge before the expiration of that time. The lodge cannot restore in either case except by a two-thirds vote. (Const. of G. L., Art. 6, Sec. 4.)

A suspended brother may petition his lodge for restoration without recommendation, but to claim the favorable consideration of the lodge it is better to be recommended. (Decisions of G. M., No. 82.)

The lodge cannot restore from expulsion except upon petition of the delinquent, with good recommendation. A unanimous vote is required for such restoration. (Const. of G. L., Art. 6, Sec. 4.) Precisely the same steps must be taken as upon the election of a profane. The man under sentence of expulsion, although in possession of Masonic knowledge, is nevertheless, in contemplation of Masonic law, as much a stranger to the fraternity as though he had never been initiated, passed nor raised. He has no Masonic existence whatever; and his restoration is, in legal effect, the making of a new Mason.

An expelled offender cannot be restored upon his verbal application merely; he must petition in writing, setting forth his present standing and his desire for restoration, and his willing determination to abide henceforth by the rules of the Order. A petition for restoration, whether it be from one under sentence of suspension or expulsion, can only be presented to and received by the lodge wherein the trial was had and sentence passed, or the Grand Lodge within whose jurisdiction said lodge was held.

PETITION FOR RESTORATION.

To the Worshipful Master, Wardens and Brethren of......Lodge, No..., of Free and Accepted Masons.

The undersigned respectfully represents that he was formerly a member of said lodge. That on or about the......day of......A. L. 58..., he was tried for unmasonic conduct upon charges preferred against him in said lodge, and that upon due conviction of said charges the said lodge passed sentence of......against him, which sentence is now in full force and effect.

That he is desirous of being restored to the rights and benefits of Masonry, and to his membership in said lodge, and he hereby solemnly promises upon his honor that if such restoration shall be granted him, he will ever yield a cheerful obedience to all the laws, rules and customs of the fraternity.

Wherefore he respectfully prays the said lodge to restore him to his Masonic rights and membership as aforesaid.

Dated......A. L. 58...

A......... B.........

Recommended by
S......... T.........
U......... V.........

No subordinate lodge except the one that passed the sentence is competent to restore from any of the disabilities attending the same.

Restoration can only be made at a regular communication, and while the lodge is open upon the third degree. It cannot lawfully occur at any special communication, even though the same be called for that purpose.

The vote upon restoration from sentence of expulsion must be by ballot, which ballot is subject to the same rules as if cast for initiation.

Unconditional restoration from sentence of expulsion, if made by a subordinate lodge, restores the delinquent to all the rights he enjoyed at the time of his expulsion. If, at the time of his expulsion, he was a member of the lodge, it restores him both to Masonry and to membership; if he was not a member, it restores him to Masonry only. But restoration from expulsion does not in any case restore to office; for by the sentence all personal and official rights are not simply suspended, but utterly destroyed, and nothing but a new election can re-invest the party with official power.

Restoration by *act of the Grand Lodge* takes place upon appeal or upon petition.

It has already been remarked, in the chapter upon Masonic Penalties, that the sentence or decision of the lodge stands in full force in all cases, until formally revoked by the Grand Lodge. But if, upon the trial of an appeal, the sentence of expulsion or suspension passed in the lodge be reversed by the Grand Lodge, such reversal reverts to the very root of the matter, and annuls the sentence from the beginning; so that the case then stands as though no sentence had ever been passed. Reversal of conviction and sentence upon appeal, has precisely the same legal effect as a judgment of acquittal would have had if passed by the lodge in the first instance. It therefore follows as an inevitable result, that upon judgment of reversal being passed by the Grand Lodge as aforesaid, the accused stands completely justified, and is at once re-invested with all his rights. He is perfectly restored, both to Masonry and to membership. Deprivation of membership was one of the results of the sentence; and as that sentence stands absolutely revoked and annulled, all of its results are revoked and annulled with it. The effect cannot continue without the cause. To still debar him of membership, would be to inflict punishment upon a man whom the highest judicial authority has pronounced entirely innocent. A lodge can no more deprive a Mason of his membership without legal and sufficient reason, than of his general Masonic rights. It is true that each lodge has the absolute right to admit to or exclude from its membership whomsoever it pleases, without dictation from the Grand Lodge; but this is not obliging the lodge to *admit* a member who is distasteful to it; it is only saying to the lodge, "you shall not unlawfully and unjustly *eject* a member whom you have freely admitted among your number." The question is purely judicial in its nature, and does not touch at all the right of the lodge to admit or reject whoever it pleases; for *re*jection and *e*jection are widely different things. The action which a lodge takes in passing judgment and sentence in a Masonic trial, and the action which it takes in balloting upon a petition for membership or initiation, are as dissimilar as the action of a court and of a legislative body. There is therefore no real conflict between this righteous and well-supported principle, and the principle of that independent control which the lodge has over the question of membership, as some have vainly argued. Besides, the very jurisdiction which the Grand Lodge has of the appeal, necessarily presupposes and implies the authority to determine all matters connected therewith.

In combating the erroneous opinion, advanced by some, that such a reversal reinstates the accused in

Masonry only, and not in his membership, Dr. Mackey observes: "Who will dare to say that a lodge may thus, by an arbitrary exercise of power, inflict this grievous wrong on a brother, and that the Grand Lodge has not the prerogative, as the supreme protector of the rights of the whole fraternity, to interpose its superior power, and give back to injured innocence all that iniquity or injustice would have deprived it of? Who will dare to say, in the face of the great principles of justice and equity, that though innocent, a Mason shall receive but a portion of the redress to which he is entitled, and that he shall be sent from the interposing shield of the supreme authority and highest court of justice of the Order, not protected in his innocence and restored to his rights, but as an innocent man, sharing in the punishment which should only have been awarded to the guilty? A doctrine so full of arbitrary oppression and injustice would be to every honest man the crying reproach of the institution."

That eminent civil and Masonic jurist, Albert Pike, in commenting upon this question, says: "If, in case of trial and conviction, suspension or expulsion from the rights and benefits of Masonry is adjudged, that includes, as a part of itself, suspension or expulsion from membership. If, on appeal, the Grand Lodge reverses the decision of the subordinate, on the ground of error in the proceedings, or of innocence, that reversal *annuls* the judgment, and it is as if never pronounced. Consequently it has *no effect whatever;* and, in Masonic law, the matter stands as if no such judgment had ever been rendered. The effect of reversal is, that the accused was never suspended nor expelled at all, in law; and there is no power in the Grand Lodge, either by judgment or by previous legislation, to give such judgment or reversal any other or less effect. These principles of Masonic law seem to us so palpably plain and correct as to need no argument; and if violated anywhere, we hope to see the ancient landmarks set up again in this respect."

The Grand Lodge restores, in the second instance, upon the petition of one who is under sentence of expulsion or suspension, where the legality or justice of the sentence is not denied. In this case it is not redress against the wrongful act of an inferior tribunal that is asked, or granted, but a favor proceeding out of the clemency and grace of the supreme power. It is in the nature of a pardon, or remission of a penalty lawfully imposed, based upon the fact that the party has abandoned his wickedness, and given assurance, by evident reformation, of honorable conduct for the future.

In this case the Grand Lodge may, by its prerogative of mercy, restore the petitioner to the rights and benefits of Masonry, but not to his membership in any lodge. The reason of this is evident. The sentence having never been questioned nor revoked, nor its justice denied, the petitioner stands totally deprived of his Masonic rights and membership. He comes not in the character of an appellant, but of a stranger; not as a litigant within the Order, but as a stranger from without. His Masonic rights and his membership being utterly lost, or completely suspended, a *new admission* must be granted by the appropriate jurisdiction before he can again enjoy either. The Grand Lodge has power to invest him with the rights and benefits of Masonry, but not to admit to membership in any lodge. Only by consent of the lodge itself can new members be admitted into its own body. The Masonic standing of a brother thus restored by the Grand Lodge is, therefore, that of an unaffiliated Mason; and he may petition and be admitted to membership in the lodge; for it is against the spirit of Masonry to encourage or enforce non-affiliation.

Thus it will be seen that a very material difference exists between restoration upon appeal and upon petition to the Grand Lodge. In fact, the former can scarcely, in strict propriety, be denominated a *restoration,* though it is invariably treated under that title: it is rather the nullifying or setting aside of an unlawful or unjust sentence; whereas the latter is founded upon the express admission that the original sentence was lawful and just. The former removes every deprivation, both of fraternity and membership; the latter restores to Masonry, but not to membership. The former is granted as a matter of justice; the latter as a matter of grace. The former is judicial; the latter is non-judicial. The former moves to a litigant brother within the Order; the latter to a petitioning stranger without.

The Grand Lodge has equal power to restore, whether the sentence be that of a subordinate lodge, or its own; and whether it be that of expulsion, or of definite or indefinite suspension.

A petition to the Grand Lodge for restoration should be substantially the same as that to a subordinate lodge, a form for which is given in a former part of this chapter. It should specify the former standing and membership of the petitioner, the lodge wherein he was tried, the nature and date of the sentence, his purpose to abide by the rules of the Order, and close with a prayer for restoration. The address should be to the Grand Lodge by its official title, and the recommendation should be by at least two members or officers of the Grand Lodge, with an avouchment by the Master or Secretary of the lodge by which the sentence was passed.

XIV.

OF GRAND LODGE TRIALS.

The Grand Lodge is a representative body, composed of its own Grand Officers, Past Grand Masters who are members of subordinate lodges, the Worshipful Masters of chartered lodges, or such representatives as may occasionally be appointed in the room of Masters unable to attend. All Past Masters of subordinate lodges, who are in good standing, are honorary members of the Grand Lodge, without the right to vote. (Const. of G. L., Art. 1, Sec. 2.) It is hailed by the style and title of "THE GRAND LODGE OF FREE AND ACCEPTED MASONS OF THE STATE OF MICHIGAN." (Ibid. Art. 1, Sec. 1.)

Our Grand Lodge is a body corporate under the laws of the State of Michigan, with full power to sue and be sued, purchase, hold or grant real and personal estate, make contracts, enact by-laws and regulations, and do all other things which private corporations may of right do. (Laws of Mich., 1849, page 313; Do., 1869, page 115.)

Its jurisdiction is co-extensive with the limits of the State, and within said jurisdiction it is the supreme Masonic authority. Its powers are plenary and absolute, except as they are limited by the ancient and immutable Landmarks of Freemasonry (Gen. Reg. of 1721, No. 39); its corporate and civil powers being of course limited by the legislative acts of incorporation. It holds a general supervisory control of the craft, and faithful allegiance and implicit obedience are due to it from all subordinate lodges and individual Masons within its jurisdiction.

The Masonic functions of the Grand Lodge are usually considered under three heads, viz:

1. The Legislative.
2. The Executive.
3. The Judicial.

Only the judicial branch of its powers is properly within the scope of this treatise, and hence the legislative and executive departments will not be here considered; the reader being referred, for information upon those topics, to those works in which the general system of Masonic jurisprudence is elaborated.

As the supreme judicial authority, the Grand Lodge has both *appellate* and *original* jurisdiction. Its appellate jurisdiction extends, with certain exceptions, to the acts and decisions of every Masonic body, tribunal and officer beneath it, and has been already sufficiently considered under the title of Appeals.

The original jurisdiction of the Grand Lodge is

either *exclusive* or *concurrent.* It is exclusive over subordinate lodges and Masters of lodges, in questions between different lodges, and in the interpretation and enforcement of its own constitution, by-laws and regulations within its own body, and among its own officers and agents. It is concurrent with that of the subordinate lodges over all Masons, affiliant and non-affiliant, (except the Grand Master) within its territorial limits, and in the construction and enforcement of the general laws of Masonry. Although it is the common practice for all trials within the purview of such concurrent jurisdiction to have their inception in the subordinate lodge, and although this practice is, except in some peculiar cases, by far the more expedient, yet the Grand Lodge may at all times exercise its original jurisdiction. In brief, the original jurisdiction of the Grand Lodge, as to all judicial matters, and matters of Masonic discipline, is universal within its territorial limits, except for violations of the particular by-laws and internal regulations of subordinate lodges; in which case each lodge has exclusive original jurisdiction, from which appeals lie to the Grand Lodge.

The Grand Lodge has exclusive penal jurisdiction over the Grand Master, to be exercised according to such regulations as shall be prescribed by the Grand Lodge itself. (Gen. Reg. of 1721, No. 19.) But, with honor to our Grand Masters be it said, there has never yet been an instance where such interposition has been necessary; every Grand Master

E

having borne himself in a manner worthy of the dignity of his high office.

Charges against a lodge or a Worshipful Master can only be preferred to the Grand Lodge, or, in the *interim*, to the Grand Master, and are framed upon the same general principles as charges preferred in a subordinate lodge against an individual Mason.

CHARGES AGAINST A LODGE.

To the M. W. Grand Lodge of Free and Accepted Masons of the State of Michigan.

......Lodge, No..., of Free and Accepted Masons, is hereby charged with willful violation of Section 9 of Article 6 of the Constitution of said Grand Lodge, in this, to-wit:

Specification 1. That said lodge has for more than one year last past neglected to assemble.

Specification 2. That said Lodge has for two years last past neglected to make returns or pay dues to said Grand Lodge.

All of which is contrary to Masonic law, and tends to the wrong and injury of said Grand Lodge and of the craft; wherefore it is demanded that said lodge be put upon trial therefor, and dealt with according to Masonic law and usage.

Dated......A. L. 58....

C......... D........, Accuser.

CHARGES AGAINST A MASTER.

To the M. W. Grand Lodge of Free and Accepted Masons of the State of Michigan.

O...... P......, Worshipful Master of......Lodge, No. ..., of Free and Accepted Masons, is hereby charged with gross unmasonic conduct, in willfully violating

Section 14 of Article 6 of the Constitution of said Grand Lodge, in this, to-wit:

Specification 1. That the said O. P., while presiding as Worshipful Master of said lodge, at a regular communication thereof, held on the...day of......, A. L. 58..., did in open lodge use, and permit to be used by brethren there assembled, distilled spirits and intoxicating liquors.

Said O. P. is further charged with unmasonic conduct, and with a willful violation of his official duties and obligations, in this, to-wit:

Specification 2. That the said O. P. did, at a regular communication of said lodge, held on the...day of......, A. L. 58..., raise one W. F. to the sublime degree of a Master Mason, after the ballot for the advancement of the said W. F. had been inspected and declared not clear, and against the protest of the brethren.

Which acts of the said O. P. are in violation of his duties and obligations as a Mason and as a Worshipful Master, and to the scandal and disgrace of the Masonic fraternity; wherefore it is demanded that the said O. P. be put upon trial before said Grand Lodge, and dealt with according to Masonic law and usage; and it is further demanded and prayed that the M. W. Grand Master do forthwith suspend the said O. P. from his office of Worshipful Master until the next annual communication of said Grand Lodge.

Dated......A. L. 58....

C......... D........., Accuser.

The charges should be filed with the Grand Secretary. The Grand Master, upon being made acquainted with their contents, orders the issuing of summons to the accused, commanding him to appear and answer within a time prescribed in the summons, and makes such other order as the case may demand. If the charges be against a lodge, he may arrest its charter until the trial; if against a Master, he may forthwith suspend the accused from his office for a like period.

The Grand Secretary serves the summons, accompanied by any interlocutory order which the Grand Master may make, and a certified copy of the charges, upon the accused, or causes the same to be done.

ORDER OF GRAND MASTER, ARRESTING CHARTER OF LODGE.

Office of the Grand Master of Masons
of the State of Michigan.
June 13th, A. D. 18..., A. L. 58...

In the matter of......Lodge,
No..., of F. and A. Masons.

Upon the filing of charges and specifications against said lodge by R. S., and upon good cause appearing, by virtue of the power and authority in me vested as Grand Master of Masons in the State of Michigan, I do hereby order that the charter of said lodge be and the same is hereby arrested, and the opening and working of said lodge thereunder forbidden until the trial and decision of said charges and specifications by the Grand Lodge; and that the Worshipful Master of said lodge do forthwith deliver said charter to the Grand Secretary, to be by him retained, subject to such order as the Grand Lodge shall make.

Witness my hand at......, the date above written.

A. T. M., Grand Master.

ORDER OF GRAND MASTER, SUSPENDING WORSHIPFUL MASTER FROM OFFICE.

Office of the Grand Master of Masons
of the State of Michigan.
June 13th, A. D. 18..., A. L. 58...

In the matter
of
Brother O.... P....

Upon the filing of charges against Brother O. P., Worshipful Master of......Lodge, No..., of Free and Accepted Masons, and upon good cause appearing, by virtue of the power and authority in me vested as Grand Master of Masons in the State of Michigan, I do hereby order that the said O. P. be and he is hereby suspended from the functions of his office as Worshipful Master, and forbidden to exercise the same, until the trial and decision of said charges by the Grand Lodge.

Witness my hand at......, the date above written.

A. T. M., Grand Master.

The proofs are usually taken by commissioners appointed by the Grand Master or the Grand Lodge. The powers of the Grand Master in connection with a Grand Lodge trial correspond very nearly with those of a Master upon a trial in a subordinate lodge. The same general rules as to counsel, proofs and notice apply, and upon the coming in of the report of the commissioners the steps to be taken are substantially the same as in a subordinate lodge, though the particular method of procedure in any trial is entirely at the option of the Grand Lodge. All judicial action in the Grand Lodge is taken by a majority vote, which vote may be reconsidered at any time within twenty-four hours. (By-Laws of G. L. Art. 9.)

The Grand Master has power, in case of emergency, to convene the Grand Lodge specially for the purposes of a trial. No judicial action can be taken in any case unless there be present representatives from at least twenty-five subordinate working lodges. (Const. of G. L., Art. 1, Sec. 3.)

In some jurisdictions the general judicial business of the Grand Lodge, original as well as appellate, is referred to a Court of Appeals for investigation and adjudication, which is in reality only another method of trial by the Grand Lodge itself; such court being the immediate agent and referee of the Grand Lodge. The decisions of such court, being in effect the decisions of the Grand Lodge itself, are of like force as though made by that body. For further remarks in this regard the reader is referred to the chapter on Appeals.

Upon individual delinquents the Grand Lodge inflicts any of the Masonic penalties, in its discretion. A delinquent lodge is usually punished by arresting or revoking its charter.

Upon the ground of manifest error or mistake, newly discovered evidence, or other sufficient cause, the Grand Lodge may, upon application of either party, grant a new trial within its own body. If the Grand Lodge be not in session, application for new trial may be made to the Grand Master, who has in the *interim* full power to grant the same.

APPLICATION FOR NEW TRIAL.

To the M. W. Grand Lodge of Free and Accepted Masons of the State of Michigan. (Or to the M. W. Grand Master of, etc.)

The undersigned hereby requests that a new trial be granted in the matter of (here designate the case) for the following reasons, to wit:

1. Because he has discovered since the trial of said matter, and is now able to produce, the following new evidence, to wit: (Here set forth the new evidence.)

2. Because the Grand Lodge was misled, and great injury wrought to the undersigned, by the testimony of G. M., whose testimony the undersigned is now able to show by the testimony of B. W. and L. N. (or any other testimony) was false and untrue in the following particulars: (state in what particulars,) which testimony of the said G. M. the undersigned was unable to rebut at the said trial.

3. Because the Grand Lodge erred in passing judgment upon said matter when there was not a constitutional quorum present. (Here state the proof of the fact.)

4. Because the decision of the Grand Lodge was contrary to the law and the evidence in this, to wit: (specify the error.)

Dated...... A. L. 58...

A......... B.........

A new trial will not be granted by the Grand Lodge, as a general rule, unless the application therefor be made within the time limited for taking appeals from subordinate lodges; namely, ninety days from notice of judgment. But upon good cause being shown for the delay, new trial may be granted at any time; and of the sufficiency of such cause the Grand Lodge or the Grand Master is the judge.

ORDER BY GRAND MASTER FOR NEW TRIAL.

Office of the Grand Master of Masons
of the State of Michigan,
June 13th, A. D. 18..., A. L. 58...

In the matter
of
Brother A... B...

Upon application of the said A. B., and upon good cause to me shown, by virtue of the power and authority in me vested as Grand Master of Masons in the State of Michigan, I do hereby order that a new trial be had in the said matter, and that the same be brought on for hearing before the Grand Lodge at the next annual communication thereof.

And further, that a copy of this order be served upon......within......days from the date hereof.

Witness my hand at......the date above written.

A. T. M., Grand Master.

The granting of a new trial before the Grand Lodge is attended with the like effects, as to the former decision or sentence, and the Masonic standing of the accused, as in trials before a subordinate lodge; and the trial proceeds upon the same general principles as in the first instance.

SUPPLEMENTARY CHAPTER.

POWERS OF THE GRAND MASTER RELATIVE TO TRIALS AND APPEALS.

There is one other subject which, although not strictly within the purview of any of the particular divisions under which Masonic Trials are treated in the foregoing pages, is still necessary to the proper completion of a treatise of this nature; and it has accordingly been reserved for separate consideration.

The subject is that of the power of the Grand Master as pertaining to judicial matters; including the question of the legality of appeals to him in certain cases, as the presiding head of the craft. The inquiry is not without its difficulties; for notwithstanding the importance of the principles involved, a wide diversity of opinion exists among the most eminent Masonic jurists in regard to some of them; and hence occasion will be here taken to discuss with particularity some points that have been only briefly mentioned, or incidentally alluded to, in the preceding chapters.

In the chapter upon the Tribunal it has been already remarked that the only judicial tribunals known in ancient craft Masonry were Lodges and Grand Lodges. In that portion of the old York Constitutions of A. D. 926 denominated the "Fifteen Points," we find the following laid down as the tenth point: "If a Mason live amiss, or slander his brother, so as to bring the craft to shame, he shall have no further maintenance among the brethren, but shall be summoned *to the next Grand Lodge;* and if he refuse to appear, he shall be expelled." Dr. Mackey, in commenting upon the judicial powers of the Grand Lodge says: "There is no fact in the history of Masonic jurisprudence more certain than that the General Assembly, or Grand Lodge, always in ancient times exercised an original jurisdiction and supervision over the craft;" and he might have added with equal truth, that the exclusive power to hear and determine Masonic trials was anciently in the same grand body. We nowhere find, either in the Ancient Landmarks or in the Ancient Constitutions of 926, any provision recognizing or implying the existence of this power in the Grand Master, nor yet in the subordinate lodges. But by the fifth section of the Constitutions of Edward III, 1427–77, a portion of that penal jurisdiction that had before rested solely in the Grand Lodge or General Assembly, was dele-

gated to the subordinate lodges, in the words following: "That at such congregations (i. e., lodges) it shall be inquired whether any Master or Fellow has broken any of the articles agreed to. And if the offender, being duly cited to appear, prove rebel, and will not attend, then *the lodge shall determine against him* that he shall forswear (or renounce) his Masonry, and shall no more use this craft." And again, by the ninth section of the General Regulations of 1721 (which, though of comparatively modern date, are usually classed with the more ancient law of Masonry) it is provided that, "If any brother so far misbehave himself as to render his lodge uneasy, he shall be twice duly admonished by the Master or Wardens *in a formed lodge;* and if he will not refrain his imprudence, and obediently submit to the advice of the brethren, and reform what gives them offense, *he shall be dealt with according to the by-laws of that particular lodge*, or else in such a manner as the quarterly communication shall think fit; for which a new regulation may be afterwards made." But neither by the Ancient Landmarks, nor the Ancient Constitutions, nor the General Regulations of 1721, is any power to hear and determine Masonic trials conferred upon, or recognized as existing in, the Grand Master.

It is certain, then, that the only tribunals with full judicial powers that are known in ancient Freemasonry are lodges and Grand Lodges; for while it is true that Grand Lodges, as at present organized, are of comparatively modern date, (the beginning of the

18th century of the Christian era) yet from time immemorial it was the custom of the craft to convene annually, or oftener, in General Assembly; which assembly was a convocation of all Masons living within a particular district or jurisdiction, with supreme and exclusive power, when so convened, over all matters, whether legislative, executive or judicial, touching the welfare of the Order; and although our Grand Lodges are at present, for the sake of convenience and economy, composed of representatives instead of the aggregate membership of the craft, yet they are in every respect the regular and lawful successors of the former General Assemblies, and in them are vested all the powers and prerogatives of those ancient bodies, except so far as the same have been delegated to the subordinate lodges. Hence, while the Grand (and Worshipful) Masters have certain very important incidental powers pertaining to Masonic trials, yet they cannot try, sentence nor punish; and whatever action they may take in the premises is subject to review by the body whose instrument they are, namely, the Grand Lodge; for they are but the agents, in legal contemplation, of that supreme tribunal, for the administration of Masonic justice—the Grand Lodge being the sole fountain not only of justice, but also of all judicial power within the Order.

Now let us consider the powers of the Grand Master relative to appeals. The thirteenth of the Ancient Landmarks declares the inalienable "right of every Mason to appeal from the decision of his brethren in lodge convened *to the Grand Lodge,* or General Assembly of Masons." Previous to the Constitutions of Edward III. these appeals must have been only as to decisions touching the work or general business of the lodge; for until that time no Masonic trials for offenses could ever occur there; the power to hear the same not having been delegated by the General Assembly. In the thirteenth of the General Regulations of 1721 it is provided: "At the said quarterly communication all matters that concern the fraternity in general, or particular lodges, or single brethren, are quietly, sedately and maturely to be discoursed of and transacted. * * * * Here also differences that cannot be made up and accommodated privately, *nor by a particular lodge,* are to be seriously considered and decided. And if any brother thinks himself aggrieved by the decision of this board, *he may appeal to the annual Grand Lodge next ensuing,*" etc. The twenty-eighth of the same Regulations provides, as a part of the business of the Grand Lodge, "*to receive any appeals* duly lodged, as above regulated, that the appellant may be heard," etc. Here we find no power vested in the Grand Master to hear appeals, nor any right conferred of appeal to any other tribunal than the Grand Lodge. Whence, then, arises that practice (which, by long usage and wide-spread recognition, has acquired the force of law) of appealing from those decisions of the lodge pertaining to work or general business, directly to the Grand Master himself, during the recess of the Grand Lodge? Is it dependent solely upon immemorial custom for its legality? or is it based upon some positive enactment? Though appeals from the lodge to the Grand Master may be of rare occurrence in this jurisdiction, yet in many others they occur continually, and as a matter of course; and their legality is not questioned by any authority that I have been able to consult.

We find the powers of the Grand Master to be derived from two sources; namely, from prerogative and from grant. Those derived from the former source are inherent in his office, and pertain to it indefeasibly, independent of any authorization or sanction by the Grand Lodge, or by any body of Masons whatever. Those derived from the latter source are delegated to him by act of the General Assembly or Grand Lodge. In the enumeration of the several branches of the prerogative of the Grand Master we find the following, viz: "To exercise a general supervision and government of the fraternity in his jurisdiction, during the recess of the Grand Lodge." By common consent of all Masons throughout the world this has been from time immemorial an unquestioned branch of his prerogative. In the sixteenth of the General Regulations of 1721 it is provided that, "the Grand Wardens, or any others, are first to advise with the Deputy *about the affairs of the lodge* or of the brethren, and not to apply to the Grand Master without the knowledge of the Deputy,

unless he refuse his concurrence in any certain necessary affair; in which case, or in case of any difference between the Deputy and the Grand Wardens, or other brethren, both parties are to *go by concert to the Grand Master*, who can easily decide the controversy, and make up the difference by virtue of his great authority." Here we have a positive enactment, by the highest Masonic authority, which clearly and expressly contemplates the appealing of disputed questions *concerning the affairs of the lodge* to the Grand Master during the recess of the Grand Lodge. But nowhere in the circle of Masonic jurisprudence do we find any power in the Grand Master to entertain an appeal from the decision of a subordinate lodge in a *Masonic trial*, had upon charges preferred against an individual brother for a Masonic offense, and where *guilt or innocence* is the question involved; nor has his prerogative of general supervision of the craft during the recess of the Grand Lodge ever been so construed by any ancient authority. Yet the appealing of cases of this character to the Grand Master is not altogether unknown, though it is happily rare, in the United States.

After a careful consideration of the law, the following conclusions seem to be legitimate.

1. Lodges and Grand Lodges are the only tribunals having jurisdiction to try and punish for Masonic offenses.

2. The powers of Masters and Grand Masters, as pertaining to *Masonic trials*, are incidental only, and

their acts in the premises are subject to review by their superior, the Grand Lodge.

3. It is lawful to appeal to the Grand Master, in the *interim* of the Grand Lodge, upon questions relating to the general affairs and business of the lodge. (The opinions of Past Grand Master J. Adams Allen [Decisions of G. M., Nos. 30 and 35] will be found to go no further than this:) But the practice of appealing to the Grand Master from the decision of the lodge in trials for Masonic offenses, where the question of *guilt or innocence* is involved, is of extremely doubtful legality, and ought to be discouraged.

4. That from the decision of the Grand Master upon any appeal, or upon any question submitted to him, a final appeal may be taken to the Grand Lodge, the decision of that Grand body being alone *final* in any case.

5. That the power of the Grand Master to make any interlocutory order, as of temporary suspension from office, arrest of charter, stay of proceedings, and the like, extends equally to original cases and to cases coming up on appeal.

6. That any order which the Grand Master may make in a case will be of binding force until reviewed by the Grand Lodge; he being, during the *interim*, the temporary ruler of the craft.

I am fully aware of the great conflict of authority that exists regarding some of the propositions above laid down; but when we consider the hasty and often inconsiderate action of many of our Grand Lodges, and the unsettled condition of a large portion of our Masonic jurisprudence, the disagreement which we find among the most intelligent craftsmen is matter of but little surprise. To rehearse the arguments *pro* and *con* would be to expand this volume to ten times its intended size. After having laboriously followed the arguments and fancies of many writers, I have been content to cite only the undisputed language of the fundamental law, for upon that all true interpretation must be based.

MICHIGAN DIGEST.

DECISIONS OF THE GRAND MASTERS.

EXPLANATORY NOTE.—The following digest of decisions of the Grand Masters includes those, and those only, that have been officially reported to the Grand Lodge, and by that body formally approved in annual communication. Thus these decisions come to us, not simply as the individual opinions of the several distinguished officers by whom they were given, but also with the additional authority of the deliberate sanction and adoption of the Grand Lodge of this state; whereby they are made the law of this jurisdiction until they shall be lawfully repealed. They are the *res judicata*, the adjudged cases which stand in a like relation to our Masonic judiciary as the reported decisions of the Supreme Court of the State do to the courts of law. Although some of them are upon points so familiar as to appear almost uncalled for, yet very many of them touch questions of vital importance to the craft, and settle matters which have at times been sources of serious misunderstanding. Heretofore they have existed only in

the scattered and disconnected minutes of the Grand Lodge. By gathering them here for the first time in convenient form and order, the compiler trusts that he has done his brethren some service; and by thus placing in the hands of all, a department of our local law which before was only within reach of a very few, and by them seldom searched out in order, he believes he has contributed in some degree to lighten the arduous labors of the Grand Masters, whose patience is so often tried by the constant repetition of questions that have been already repeatedly decided.

It will be observed that the recorded decisions stand connected with the names of but a minority of our Past Grand Masters. This arises from the fact that only those whose names here appear ever reported their decisions officially to the Grand Lodge for its consideration. Past Grand Master Hon. Wm. M. Fenton was the first to set the commendable example, and it is to be regretted that all of his distinguished compeers have not in the same manner brought up their work for inspection, that it might pass the overseer's square, and stand as an example to the craft.

The decisions of our present Grand Master, M. W. Alexander T. Metcalf, are necessarily, yet reluctantly, omitted from this compilation. Many of them are of great value, and eminently worthy of his acknowledged ability; but inasmuch as they have not yet passed the ordeal of the Grand Lodge, it is thought best to withhold them until they shall receive the sanction of that body.

GRAND MASTER WM. M. FENTON.

1. A lodge can expel a non-affiliated mason. (January 12th, 1859.)

2. The Grand Master cannot grant a dispensation for the election of a Junior Warden to fill vacancy while the Master and Senior Warden remain (Ibid.)

3. The accuser is a competent witness on the trial of charges against a brother, but the accused is not. (Ibid.)

4. A rejected candidate for initiation cannot apply to another lodge within one year after his rejection without the recommendation of the lodge by which he was rejected. (Ibid.—See Art. 5, sec. 6, of Const.)

5. A ballot may be taken at a special communication for advancement to the second and third degrees, after the candidate has been elected and initiated at a regular. (Ibid.)

6. A Worshipful Master can admit or reject visiting brethren at his own discretion, without the order or assent of his lodge. (Ibid.)

GRAND MASTER J. ADAMS ALLEN.

7. A Warden of a lodge under dispensation may be elected master after the lodge receives its charter. (January 11th, 1860.)

8. The object of the ballot for the second and third degrees is to determine the candidate's proficiency in the preceding degrees, and also to ascertain whether he is still worthy. (Ibid.)

9. When the ballot for advancement to the second or third degree is found not clear, the ballot may pass at any subsequent communication when the order of balloting is announced by the Worshipful

Master, unless the by-laws provide to the contrary. (Ibid.)

10. Any candidate may be prevented from advancement to the second or third degree by the casting of a black ball, and the brother casting the same cannot be questioned as to his motives, nor can he be compelled to prefer charges against the rejected brother. The secret ballot is the Mason's inalienable right, but he is amenable to discipline for the abuse of that right, the same as for any other Masonic offense. (Ibid.)

11. The sense of the lodge in matters of business should be taken as the by-laws prescribe. If they are silent, the vote should be taken by the uplifted hand, as being in accordance with Masonic usage. (Ibid.)

12. When a petition has been presented, received and referred to a committee, it cannot be withdrawn until the committee have reported it back and the consent of the lodge is given. (Ibid.—See Sec. 8, Art. 5, of Const.)

13. The committee may report back the petition to the lodge without recommendation, but all committees are subject to the direction of the lodge. (Ibid.)

14. Neither the Worshipful Master nor the lodge may admit visitors who are excluded by Constitutional provision. (See Art. 5, sec. 13, of Const.) The term *sojourner*, as used in the Constitution, does not include non-affiliants. (Ibid.)

15. A motion to suspend a by-law cannot be entertained, unless in a mode provided for in the by-laws themselves. (Ibid.)

16. When the petition of a non-affiliant for membership has been rejected, he may renew his application at any subsequent regular communication, unless the by-laws provide otherwise. Unless charges are preferred against him he is still a Mason in good standing. Nevertheless, he must present a new petition; the first is dead, and cannot be revived by a vote of the lodge. (Ibid.)

17. Neither the Worshipful Master nor Wardens can be dimitted, unless they remove from the jurisdiction. It is not in the power of the Grand Lodge to so far innovate upon the body of Masonry as to provide for any other method of relief from the duties of those several offices. Hence any resolution which may have inadvertently, or otherwise, gone upon the records of the Grand Lodge to that effect, is null and void. (Ibid.)

18. A brother Treasurer cannot refuse to pay out the funds in his hands, on due order; neither can he pay a claim of his own without consent of the lodge. His private account must take the same course with others. He has no peculiar claims. (Ibid.)

19. A brother under charges for unmasonic conduct may vote in the lodge while under such charges, upon all matters not involved in the charges against him. He is presumed innocent till proven guilty. (Ibid.)

20. An appeal to the Grand Lodge does not restore the appellant to the rights and privileges of his lodge until decision thereupon. If this were not the case, the party convicted might set all decisions of his own lodge at defiance.

21. Where the ballot is regularly passed and found not clear, a new ballot cannot be ordered upon the ground that several brethren were excused from voting. The Worshipful Master may be subject to censure for his decision, but the candidate is rejected. (Ibid.)

22. Where the brother who casts the black ball by which a candidate is rejected waives his objection, the ballot cannot for that reason be passed a third time. The petition is dead, and can only be renewed by the petitioner on consent of the lodge, or as fixed by the by-laws. (Ibid.—See Art. 5, sec. 7 of Const.)

23. A brother was present at the receiving and reference of a petition, but not at the balloting for the first degree; he was also present at the initiation, but urged no objection. Subsequently he preferred charges to prevent the candidate's advancement.

The brother was chargeable with unmasonic conduct in not objecting to the initiation of the candidate, if his objections could properly be made known. But, as charges may be preferred against a Mason, and a brother held to trial on the testimony of one not a Mason, so it is the duty of the lodge to take cognizance of charges from any respectable source, involving the character of a candidate for advancement; particularly such charges as would, if established, show his utter disqualification. The objecting brother did wrong in postponing his duty, but this can be no excuse for the lodge neglecting theirs. Neither does this conflict with the principle that a candidate elected notwithstanding known charges, ought not thereafter to be tried upon them; *the ballot is their verdict.* (Ibid.)

24. The time within which a duly elected candidate may be initiated is usually fixed by the by-laws. If not so fixed, Masonic usage must govern, which limits it to twelve months. All action under such election after that period would be unlawful. The parties are then free from any reciprocal obligations, and the election can neither be revived nor annulled. The only remedy is by filing a new petition. (Ibid.)

25. The certificate of the Worshipful Master, or Secretary, in the absence of entry upon the approved records of the lodge, is not sufficient evidence of the transactions of the lodge. A lodge is bound by the records which it has duly approved, and no further. It has power to amend its records, upon such evidence as is deemed sufficient; and such amended record, duly attested, has all the force and effect of an original record. But neither the Grand Lodge nor sister lodges are warranted in receiving as evidence to control their action, statements or allegations from any source, presuming the inaccuracy of said records; unless, indeed, the lodge be put upon trial before the

Grand Lodge for falsifying its records, which brings up quite another matter. (Ibid.)

26. A general charge of unmasonic conduct, written with a pencil, and without specifications, preferred against a brother applying for a dimit, ought not to be entertained by the Worshipful Master. Pencil writing, if clear and distinct, may be admissible, but as a general rule in matters of such Masonic importance it should be excluded. A loose, vague and general charge of misconduct ought not to be received even in writing. If the case appears one of probability, the Master may direct the usual steps to be taken and specific charges preferred. (Ibid.)

27. The accuser need not be put under oath. Masonry regards no obligation to speak the truth more binding than its own. (Ibid.)

28. A dimit takes effect immediately on the declaration of the vote by the W. M., if called for in open lodge; if not, immediately on the approval of the minutes. The Secretary's certificate is not in itself a dimit, as it is loosely denominated; it may never be called for, and yet the dimission be complete. (Ibid.)

29. The ballot should be so conducted as to secure absolute secresy. Each lodge is at liberty to determine how, in its own case, that object can be best secured. (Ibid.)

30. A motion to appeal from the W. M. to the lodge, is unmasonic, and out of order. The W. M. is prohibited from entertaining the motion even by courtesy. The decision of the W. M. is only to be

met by an appeal to the Grand Lodge, or, in the *interim*, to the Grand Master. The W. M. is responsible to the Grand Lodge or the Grand Master *only*. A lodge has no power to insert a provision in its by-laws for an appeal from the W. M. to the lodge. (Ibid.)

31. It is not competent for a lodge to insert in its by-laws a provision for a motion of the "previous question," or to "adjourn." It is the duty of the W. M. to "order the work," control debate within proper limits, and close the lodge at his will and pleasure; subject only to his obligations, and the will and decision of the Grand Lodge. (Ibid.)

32. Any degree of mutilation or dismemberment that will prevent a candidate from assuming the proper positions, and giving expression to the appropriate and necessary methods of recognition well known to the fraternity, will disqualify him as a candidate for Masonry. Dismemberment of a foot or right hand is a disqualification. Immobility of the knee joints is equally so. A candidate should be in the full possession of all his members and faculties as a sound man ought to have. (Ibid.)

33. The lodge may determine the mode of election for honorary membership, but if the ballot be chosen it should be remembered that the effect is not the same as an original ballot for initiation, as it may be reconsidered. It is not proper for a lodge to elect a non-affiliating Mason an honorary member. (Ibid.)

34. Any vote or resolution may be reconsidered,

and such action taken as the lodge shall see fit. This language, of course, *does not include reconsideration of the ballot.* (Ibid.)

35. The W. M. has power to refuse the passage of the ballot box for the second or third degrees, against the wishes of the majority of the lodge; but he is responsible for the abuse of this power to the Grand Lodge, or, in the *interim,* to the Grand Master, and to them only. (Ibid.)

36. A Master elect need not have received the degree of Past Master in order to his being installed and presiding over a lodge. The Grand Lodge of Michigan knows nothing of the Past Master's degree, so called. The qualifications for the Mastership are fully set forth in the Grand Constitution, and none other are required. (Ibid.)

37. When an Entered Apprentice or Fellow Craft, applying for advancement, is black balled, he may renew his application at any regular communication, unless charges of unmasonic conduct are preferred against him, when he must of course await the decision of the lodge. (Ibid.)

38. A lodge under dispensation can only exercise those powers which are specifically granted. Hence, in this jurisdiction, it may *admit,* but cannot dimit members. (Ibid.)

39. If an Entered Apprentice, after initiation proves himself unworthy, he should be prevented from advancing by direction of the W. M. or by the black ball. The W. M. should direct formal charges

to be made against him, and on conviction he may receive such censure or discipline as the circumstances indicate. (Ibid.)

40. "Calling off" from one communication to another is especially prohibited. In all cases the lodge must be opened and closed in form. (Ibid.)

41. If not otherwise provided in the by-laws, the presence of the W. M. or either of the Wardens, with two brethren of the lodge, at a regular communication, is sufficient for the transaction of business, balloting, etc. (Ibid.

42. Visiting brethren may be set at work *on the level* with members of the lodge, but cannot vote. They may, by permission of the W. M., guard the South and West, carry directions, orders, etc., but may not properly preside in the East except as the temporary agents of the W. M. (Ibid.)

43. A brother who is in the habit of gross intoxication is neither fit for Tiler nor for Masonic fraternity, inside or outside of the lodge. When complaint of such conduct is made against any officer, the W. M. ought at once to suspend him from his office, and instruct the Junior Warden to prefer appropriate charges, and deal with him thereafter as the case may require. (Ibid.)

44. A lodge under dispensation has territorial jurisdiction upon all such matters as are expressly granted to it in its dispensation, and no further. It has no disciplinary power over Masons in its geographical jurisdiction, save by express grant. (Ibid.)

45. A dispensation may be granted enabling a lodge to elect a brother to the office of W. M. who has not served as a Warden, upon competent reasons shown. (Ibid.)

46. A Worshipful Master has no right to know how a brother casts his ballot, much less to ask his reasons therefor. If the brother gives his reasons, and only one black ball appear, the W. M. has no right to overrule the objection and declare the candidate elected. Under such circumstances the candidate is rejected. (Ibid.)

47. A brother who has served as a Warden in a foreign jurisdiction is eligible to the office of W. M. in this. Mastership or Wardenship, wherever Freemasonry extends, is sufficient to answer the requirements of this jurisdiction. (Ibid.)

48. A brother who has been expelled may obtain a new trial by exhibiting satisfactory reasons therefor to the Grand Lodge or Grand Master, who may thereupon order a new trial. But the lodge can only grant a new trial by an unanimous vote.

49. Honorary membership confers the right of visiting and of speaking, but not of voting nor holding office in the lodge. (Ibid.)

50. An attorney, who is a Mason, is not chargeable with unmasonic conduct if, in instituting legal proceedings against a brother, affiliant or non-affiliant, he does not forewarn the brother of the same. He has no right to prejudice the lawful interests of his

client, which might be the case in numerous instances, if the opposite rule should prevail. (Ibid.)

51. The festivals of the Saints John are regular communications. Section 1 of Art. 5 of the Constitution of our Grand Lodge recognizes them as such by necessary implication from the language employed. The ballot may pass upon the petition of a candidate upon either of said festivals, provided it be more than ten days after the same was referred. (Ibid.)

52. Charges of unmasonic conduct should be preferred against brethren who are able and will not pay their dues, and such discipline enforced as the case may require or the by-laws provide. This is by far the preferable course, and most Masonic. (Ibid.)

GRAND MASTER FRANCIS DARROW.

53. The Grand Lodge of Michigan cannot legally grant warrants or charters to any body of brethren to form and open lodges, make Masons, or in any way to interefere within the jurisdiction of any sister Grand Lodge. Upon the maintenance of this principle between our Grand Lodges depend their peace and harmony; and I have therefore refused all applications for letters of dispensation to form and open Military Lodges in regiments beyond the limits of this state. (January 8th, 1862.)

GRAND MASTER LOVELL MOORE.

54. It is not proper to recognize as Masons persons who have received the degrees in military lodges

working beyond the jurisdiction of the Grand Lodge from which they received their dispensation, nor to admit such persons into our lodges upon their passing the usual examination. They were not made in a "regularly constituted lodge." No Grand Lodge or Grand Master can legally grant a dispensation to form a lodge and make Masons within the jurisdiction of another Grand Lodge. (January 11th, 1865.)

55. The requisites of a petition to the Grand Master for a special dispensation to confer degrees are as follows, viz: it should be under the seal of the lodge, and be signed by the W. M., or by the Secretary by his order; the name, age, residence and occupation of the candidate, and the reasons why a dispensation is deemed necessary, should all be fully stated, and the Constitutional Grand Lodge fee, as specified in the Blue Book, should be enclosed, or the Grand Secretary's certificate for the same. (Ibid.)

56. A special dispensation to confer degrees, or for the formation of a new lodge, granted by the Grand Master, need not be under the seal of the Grand Lodge nor be attested by the Secretary. According to ancient usage the official signature and private seal of the Grand Master is all that is necessary in either case, it being his official executive act, and not the act of the Grand Lodge. (Ibid.)

57. Where a special dispensation has been granted to confer degrees, and the candidate is afterwards rejected, he is not entitled to have the dispensation fee refunded. (Ibid.)

58. The dispensing power is one of the prerogatives of the Grand Master by ancient usage, and he cannot delegate it to another. He alone is made the sole judge of the expediency of every particular case. (Ibid.)

59. A candidate must be physically so perfect that he can readily place himself in every position required in conferring or receiving the several degrees, and performing all the work of the lodge. (Ibid.)

60. The Grand Master cannot under any circumstances grant a dispensation for the initiation of a candidate under twenty-one years of age. (Ibid.)

61. A lodge would not be justified under any circumstances in re-initiating one who had been regularly initiated in another jurisdiction, for the purpose of avoiding the necessity of procuring permission from the lodge where he was first initiated for them to finish their work by passing and raising the candidate; neither can the Grand Master grant dispensation for that purpose. (Ibid.)

62. Where A is elected and duly installed as W. M., serves one year, is then superseded by B, then re-elected as W. M., it is necessary that A should be again installed before he again assumes the prerogatives of W. M. (Ibid.)

63. Where one is elected and installed as W. M., officiates one year, and is then re-elected, it is not absolutely necessary that he should be re-installed. (Ibid.)

64. A lodge has no right to *initiate* a candidate if, at

the time of initiation, he resides within the accredited jurisdiction of another lodge; but having been initiated, no matter where he removes to, it is the right of the lodge where he was initiated to finish their work by conferring the other degrees; and no other lodge can deprive them of that right without their consent. (Ibid.)

65. Where a candidate is balloted for under a special dispensation, and is rejected, the W. M. cannot call another special communication and receive and act upon another petition of said candidate by virtue of the same dispensation. Both the petition to the lodge and the dispensation have, by such rejection, become null and void. (Ibid.)

66. If, after a candidate is initiated, it be discovered that he has no sense of hearing on the right side, and never had, he is thereby disqualified from taking any further degrees; but what has been done cannot be undone. (Ibid.)

67. Where the ballots were cast for the election of a candidate and found *not clear*, and all the brethren said it was a mistake, and that they all intended to vote in the affirmative, the candidate is nevertheless rejected, and the petition is dead. The only remedy is to commence *de novo*. A dispensation could not reach the case. (Ibid.)

68. The prerogatives of a lodge between the time of receiving its charter from the Grand Lodge and the time of being constituted, are as follows, viz: it may meet, open, elect officers under the provisions of

an edict from the Grand Lodge for that purpose, and then close. It cannot meet at any other time, nor do any other business; its officers have no legal existence until they are installed, and those persons named in the charter can alone act for the purposes of said election. (Ibid.)

69. One who has been initiated, and then loses his right arm in battle, can take no further degrees. (Ibid.)

70. The W. M. may call a special communication by giving general notice; it need not be in writing, but should specify the particular business to be done. (Ibid.)

71. A candidate who has been once rejected should not be again balloted for except at a regular, or at a special after due notice to all the members specifying the object of the meeting. (Ibid.)

72. Balloting at a special, for a candidate rejected at a regular communication, is illegal. (Ibid.)

73. The necessary requisites of a petition for a dispensation for the formation of a new lodge are as follows, viz: it must be drawn in the usual form, and must set forth the *name* of the proposed lodge, and the *town* and *county* where it is to be located; it must be signed by at least *eight* Master Masons, and be sent to the address of the Grand Master or the Grand Secretary; it must be accompanied with the constitutional Grand Lodge fee, the recommendation of and distance from the nearest lodge, and the dimits of all the petitioners, showing that they are all Mas-

ter Masons in good and regular standing. The G. V. and L., or some other prominent Master Mason, must also certify that the three first officers are competent to discharge the duties of their respective offices and to instruct their subordinates, and that they have, or can procure, a *good, safe* lodge-room. (Ibid.)

GRAND MASTER SALATHIEL C. COFFINBURY.

74. A Senior Warden has no right to call a special communication of the lodge, open the same and proceed to work, when the W. M. is at home in the same village. (January 9th, 1867.)

75. When a summons has been served upon a brother with a copy of the charges for unmasonic conduct, and a copy of both left with the accused, it is not necessary that the seal of the lodge be impressed on the copy of the summons in order to make the service valid. The copy is supposed to be made by the officer who serves the process, and who, not having the custody of the seal, could not attach it. (Ibid.)

76. A man who has a hare lip, which, by surgical process has been closed, but who cannot articulate so as to be understood except by those well acquainted with him, cannot be made a Mason. (Ibid.)

77. When the Master of a lodge learns to his certain knowledge that a candidate, after he has been elected, and before his initiation, is unworthy to be made a Mason, his duty is, first, to refuse to initiate

the candidate, second, to inform the candidate in a courteous manner that he cannot be admitted, third, to see that the fee accompanying the petition of the candidate be refunded to him in due season.

As a general rule, the fee becomes the property of the lodge upon the election of the candidate; but, as the candidate advances his fee with the expectation of receiving value therefor from the lodge, and as the lodge refuses to return such value, it is unjust to retain the fee; and justice is one of the cardinal virtues of Masonry. (Ibid.)

78. A member of a lodge may be put upon trial before his lodge upon charges of unlawful carnal intercourse with a female who is in no wise related to a Master Mason. A man who is guilty of violation of the moral law or the statute law is guilty of unmasonic conduct, and ought to be disciplined therefor by his lodge. (Ibid.)

79. An Attorney at Law is not liable to Masonic punishment for giving legal advice against a brother Master Mason, when he knows such Master Mason is guilty of crime and unworthy to be called a brother. An attorney's duty to his client is paramount. He must give correct legal advice. I know of no rule of Masonic usage which prohibits a Mason, being an Attorney at Law, from taking a fee and conducting a suit against a brother Master Mason. A Master Mason is not bound, in any instance, to protect or shield a brother in wrong, or dishonesty, more especially in crime. (Ibid.)

80. *Question.* Can a candidate for initiation be considered as having resided within the required jurisdiction of a lodge the six months as required by sec. 6 of Art. 5 of the Constitution, who so lived three months last year and three months this, without any permanent place of residence between the two periods?

Answer. If it were the intention of the candidate to permanently reside at the given place where he resided the first three months, and he was absent visiting or on business during the intervening period, and again returns in pursuance of his first intention, his petition ought to be received; but if, after a three months' residence, he left without any intention to return, and then formed a *new intention*, and returned, his petition ought not to be received until six months after such return. (January 9th, 1868.)

81. Where a committee reports a petitioner unworthy, the candidate cannot be declared rejected without a ballot. The lodge may, by a two-thirds vote, permit the candidate to withdraw his petition without prejudice, or may require the ballot to be passed. If the former course is taken, the candidate may apply again at any time, while a rejection interdicts a second petition for a given period. (Ibid.)

82. A suspended brother may petition his lodge for restoration without recommendation, but to claim the favorable consideration of the lodge it is better to be recommended. (Ibid.)

83. A Mason under sentence of suspension may be tried by his lodge for offenses committed subsequent to the sentence, or for a repetition of the offense for which he was suspended, and if found guilty, may be expelled. It is not necessary that the delinquent be reinstated in order to enable the lodge to take this action. (Ibid.)

84. A brother who has been raised or admitted to membership upon dimit, subsequent to the sentence of suspension, is competent to sit upon any committee of the lodge, and to vote on all questions arising before the lodge while acting either in a parliamentary or judicial capacity. (Ibid.)

85. A suspended brother cannot be admitted into the lodge; he must therefore appear by agent or attorney, and such agent or attorney must be a Master Mason. If the accused do not so appear, it is the duty of the W. M. to appoint a member of the lodge as such agent or attorney, whose duty it becomes to see that the trial is fairly conducted, and the rights of the accused not imperiled. (Ibid.)

86. Whatever may be the relation of an unaffiliated Mason to our Order, he has no rights in connection with our lodges. He has not the right of visitation of a lodge, except three times by special permission; therefore he can have *no right to prefer charges against a member of a lodge,* nor has he a right to appear as counsel or attorney for a brother under charges. The position of a voluntarily unaffiliated Mason is such as he himself has sought, and he must therefore

submit to its consequences and embarrassments. (Ibid.)

87. A member who declares his intention of preventing any more initiations in the lodge, and in pursuance of such intention black-balls every petitioner, whereby the best citizens are rejected, and the prosperity of the lodge greatly embarrassed, is guilty of unmasonic conduct. Charges should be preferred against him; he should be tried thereon, and, if found guilty, suspended or expelled as the lodge may determine. (Ibid.)

88. It is the privilege of any member, at any stage of advancement of a candidate, to secretly cast a black ball when the ballot is passed. He need not assign his reason for so doing, and ought not to disclose who cast the black ball. Here ends the law.

It is the duty of every Mason who knows an advancing brother to be guilty of unmasonic conduct to prefer charges against him if he can make proof of his guilt; if, however, he is unable to make such proof, all he can do is to cast his black ball, and this, in such case, it is his duty to do. (Ibid.)

89. According to the usages, rules and general practice of Masonry, dimitted Masons cannot be accepted into a lodge while working under dispensation; but by virtue of a special edict of our Grand Lodge they may. (Ibid.)

90. The Worshipful Master has the right, after charges have been preferred in writing, and after examining them carefully, to declare them insufficient

and refuse to proceed to trial upon them. He ought not to entertain frivolous charges, or such as do not show clearly, if proven, a Masonic misdemeanor. (Ibid.)

91. If the W. M. is in doubt as to the sufficiency or competency of charges, it is proper for him to take the opinion of his lodge upon that subject by a vote. But such opinion is merely advisory, and is of no legal force upon the W. M., who is alone responsible in the premises. He is acting as the presiding head of a judicial tribunal. (Ibid.)

92. A subordinate lodge (unless it be under the Act of the State Legislature of 1865) has no legal corporate existence, and therefore cannot be seized of real estate. The Grand Lodge of Michigan is by legislative enactment a body corporate and politic, and perpetual in its existence as such. It can legally become seized of real estate, and can legally grant and convey the same.

The best method, therefore, for a subordinate lodge to become seized of real estate is as follows, viz: let the subordinate lodge take a deed from the grantor to the Grand Lodge, in trust for the use and benefit of its subordinate (which the Grand Lodge recognizes as a legitimate body, although not recognized by the law as a legal body) and for no other purpose, except that of conveyance on request of the subordinate. This vests the title in the Grand Lodge for certain purposes, and divests the grantor of all estate in the realty. Should the subordinate desire to sell or exchange, let it send a deed to the Grand Master, the legal executive head of the Grand Lodge, at any time, and his execution of it would convey the real estate to the grantee named in the deed. (January 13th, 1869.)

93. A Mason cannot, in form, resign his membership of the Order, withdraw himself from its duties, nor discharge himself from its obligations. (Ibid.)

94. A lodge has not the power to discharge a Mason from his duties as such, nor absolve him from his Masonic obligations. Could it do so at the request of a brother, the claims of the family of the brother upon the Order would remain unimpaired; for acts of either the lodge or the brother, which would compromise such claims of third parties, could have no effect against the rights of such third parties. (Ibid.)

95. A lodge cannot absolve itself and the Masonic brotherhood from their obligation to a brother except by a sentence of suspension or expulsion from all the rights and benefits of Masonry against such brother, upon a fair trial and conviction. (Ibid.)

96. A brother who will not indorse the moral theories of Masonry, and its sublime and humane lessons, and who declares that he will not be bound by its solemn obligations, ought to be expelled from all the rights and benefits of Masonry. (Ibid.)

STANDING RESOLUTIONS,

ORDERS AND EDICTS

OF THE

GRAND LODGE OF MICHIGAN.

---

1. *Resolved,* That no presiding officer in any subordinate lodge, within the jurisdiction of this Grand Lodge, is entitled to wear any other regalia, except that of a Master Mason; and any attempt to introduce any other is an innovation upon the long established usages of Masonry, and one that cannot receive the sanction of this Grand Lodge, and is hereafter expressly prohibited.

2. *Resolved,* As the opinion of this Grand Lodge, that any Master Mason in good standing, within the accredited jurisdiction of any subordinate lodge, and not a member thereof, or of any other lodge, or been rejected by any other lodge, may become a member

of any lodge within the jurisdiction of this Grand Lodge, if the lodge applied to shall see proper to receive him.

3. *Resolved,* That the W. M., or representative of each subordinate lodge which shall be represented in this Grand Lodge, the Grand Officers for the time being, and Past Grand Masters in attendance, be allowed ten cents per mile for traveling fees, computing one way only by the most usually traveled route; and three dollars per day for the time he shall actually attend the sitting of the Grand Lodge, not to be paid until the close of the communication.

Provided, That no representative shall be paid a greater amount than the lodge he represents shall have paid into the funds of the Grand Lodge, for the current year, for dues. And provided, also, that no representative be paid as the representative of more than one lodge.

4. *Resolved,* That it is necessary for a Master Mason, when elected to preside over a lodge, before entering upon the duties of his office, to receive a proper qualification, and that qualification shall be to bind him faithfully and impartially to discharge the duties of a Master of a lodge, together with the ancient charges and regulations, as laid down in Webb's Free Mason's Monitor, as compiled by R. W. Bro. James Fenton, Grand Secretary, and nothing more; and that any present or past Master, who has received the aforesaid qualifications, be authorized to perform said ceremony when requested.

5. *Resolved,* That the Grand Lodge respectfully recommend to the M. W. Grand Master that no new lodge be hereafter organized within the distance of ten miles of any other lodge now at work within this jurisdiction, unless for special causes shown.

6. *Resolved,* That every brother ought to be a member of some lodge.

7. *Resolved,* That the Grand Treasurer be, and he is hereby authorized and fully empowered, in the name of the Grand Lodge of Free and Accepted Masons of the State of Michigan, to collect, by legal proceedings or otherwise, any debt due the Grand Lodge, whenever in his opinion the interest of the Grand Lodge shall require such action.

8. *Resolved,* That this Grand Lodge will not grant a Charter to a new lodge, unless the petition shall be accompanied with a certificate from the M. W. Grand Master, or the R. W. Grand Visitor and Lecturer, showing that the three first officers thereof are competent and duly qualified to perform the work required of them respectively, and that they are conversant with the ancient charges and landmarks, and not without satisfactory evidence that they have or can secure a suitable place for holding meetings.

9. *Resolved,* That the following Masonic clothing and insignia be established as the standard in this jurisdiction; and that all lodges and brethren, hereafter procuring new clothing, be recommended to

have the same made in conformity with the following description, to wit:

JEWELS. The Jewels of the Grand Lodge, as well as of subordinate lodges, shall be the same as are now in use, of a pattern to be found in the Grand Secretary's office.

COLLARS. Of officers of subordinate lodges, to be of light blue ribbon or velvet, four inches broad.

The collar of the Grand Master shall be of purple, four inches broad, with narrow edge of gold lace, embroidered with acacia and pomegranate on the outside, and ornamented in the center with pomegranate embroidered in gold.

Other Grand Officers, present and past, wear collars of purple ribbon, four inches broad, with narrow edging of gold lace cord.

APRONS. ENTERED APPRENTICE.—A plain white lamb skin or linen, from fourteen to sixteen inches wide, twelve to fourteen inches deep, square at bottom and without ornament, white strings, with a flap or fall to be triangular in shape.

FELLOW CRAFT.—The same, with the addition only of two sky-blue rosettes at the bottom.

MASTER MASON.—The same, with sky-blue lining and edging, one and-a-half inches deep, and an additional rosette on the fall or flap, and silver tassels. No other color or ornament shall be allowed, except to officers of lodges, who may have the emblems of their office, in silver or white, in the center of the apron.

GRAND OFFICERS OF THE GRAND LODGE, PRESENT AND PAST.—Aprons of the same dimensions, lined with purple, and ornamented with gold and blue strings; they must have the emblems of their office, in gold or blue, in the center.

The apron of the Deputy Grand Master to have the emblem of his office in gold or embroidery, in the center, and the pomegranate and lotus alternately embroidered in gold on the edging.

The apron of the Grand Master is ornamented with the blazing sun, embroidered in gold, in the center; on the edging, the pomegranate and lotus, with the seven-eared wheat at each corner, and also on the fall, all in gold embroidery; the fringe of gold bullion.

The Masters and Past Masters of Lodges to wear, in lieu and in place of the three rosettes on the Master Mason's apron, perpendicular lines upon horizontal lines, thereby forming three several sets of two right angles, the length of the horizontal lines to be two inches and a half each, and of the perpendicular lines one inch; these emblems to be of ribbon or silver, half an inch broad, and, if ribbon, of the same color of the lining and edging of the apron. If Grand Officers, similar emblems, of Garter-blue or gold.

10. *Resolved,* That it is the right of all lodges working under the jurisdiction of this Grand Lodge to admit or reject visiting brethren, as they, in their discretion, may deem best.

11. (Repealed.)

12. *Resolved,* That all subordinate lodges in this jurisdiction, located on the line of States, be and they are hereby *directed* not to initiate any person who lives in any other state, without first obtaining the consent of the M. W. Grand Master of such state, and also of the W. M. of the subordinate lodge within whose jurisdiction the candidate resides.

13. *Resolved,* That the Master or Wardens of a lodge, in case of permanent removal from the jurisdiction, are entitled to a dimit, under like restrictions as other members of their lodge.

14. *Resolved,* That it is the sense of this Grand Lodge that the M. W. Grand Master should not communicate official information in reply to letters from a lodge, its officers or committees, not Masoni-

cally known to him, unless such letters are authenticated by the seal of the lodge.

15. *Resolved,* That the infliction of fines, as a penalty upon refractory committees or brothers, is inconsistent with ancient Masonic rules and usages.

16. *Resolved,* That in Masonry the accuser of a brother Mason must be a Master Mason in good standing, who need not be sworn. The complaint or testimony of persons not Masons may be taken before the examining committee, on oath or otherwise, as the lodge shall direct; but the testimony of witnesses not Masons should be taken before a committee, and not in open lodge.

17. *Resolved,* That no appeal from a subordinate lodge shall be entertained by the Grand Lodge, except upon proof that notice of said appeal has been given to the subordinate lodge in writing, within ninety days after the appellant shall have received official notice of such decision; and such appeal shall be prosecuted at the first regular communication of the Grand Lodge after the time above limited shall have expired.

18. *Resolved,* That petitions for membership may be received and acted upon, but the applicant shall not be admitted to membership until he produces his dimit, or in case of a defunct lodge, proper evidence of membership from the Grand Lodge under which the same was held. Where regular proofs cannot be obtained, such cases come within the prerogative of

the Grand Master, who may dispense therewith on proper showing, to his entire satisfaction.

19. *Resolved,* That neither three of the Masonic penalties should be inflicted upon a brother without charges, specifications, notice and trial in due Masonic form.

20. *Resolved,* That all lodges within this jurisdiction are enjoined and prohibited from encouraging, promoting or permitting the delivery or teaching any Masonic lectures or work which are not sanctioned and authorized by this Grand Lodge in accordance with its Constitution; and all brethren within this jurisdiction are prohibited from delivering or teaching such lectures to lodges in this State.

21. *Resolved,* That it is the duty of a Master of a lodge to suspend the advancement of a candidate at any stage of his advancement, when it shall come to his knowledge that such candidate is either unworthy of receiving, or ineligible to receive Masonic light, regardless of the source or channel of such knowledge.

22. *Resolved,* That all newly chartered lodges may hold their first election for officers at any regular communication within two months after the date of their charter.

23. Charges having been preferred and the committee having reported, can the accused be expelled at any but a regular communication?

[Action on the charges must be commenced at a regular communication, and may be continued from time to time and had at special communications, convened for that purpose, by vote at such regular, or notice to all the members of the lodge within the jurisdiction.]

24. It is competent to provide by the By-Laws for quarterly or annual dues, and to vote an assessment not provided for therein in cases of emergency, for relief of distressed brothers and other objects of Masonic charity, and for the necessary expenses of the lodge.

25. *Resolved,* That no lodge shall receive any petition for initiation, unless the applicant state in the petition whether he has ever applied for initiation to any other lodge, and if such application has been made, shall state the time or times when, and the lodge or lodges to which such application has been made; and in case such statements are found to be false, it shall be good cause for expulsion from the Order.

26. *Resolved,* That this Grand Lodge require all committees to whom petitions may be referred, to make a full written report, as to the character, standing and antecedents of the candidate, as well as the jurisdiction to which he may rightfully belong; and that said report be not written upon the petition itself, but upon a separate paper, signed by at least a majority of the committee, which report shall be filed in the archives of the lodge.

27. *Resolved,* That it shall be the duty of the W. M. of every subordinate lodge, to cause the Constitution and Standing Orders of this Grand Lodge to be read in their respective lodges, at least once in three months.

28. *Resolved,* That copies of the Constitution may be sold at thirty cents per copy to any brother desiring to possess one.

29. *Resolved,* That all resolutions, orders and edicts of this Grand Lodge, conflicting with the foregoing, be, and they are hereby rescinded.

30. *Resolved,* That a candidate for advancement has the right to apply at every regular communication of the lodge, unless charges have been preferred against him.

31. *Resolved,* That it is the sense of this Grand Lodge, that pursuant to Section 2, of Article 1, of the Constitution, all Past Masters of subordinate lodges, who are in good standing, are entitled to all the rights of membership in this Grand Lodge, except the right to vote.

32. *Resolved,* That any and every lodge that shall not make the required return, and pay over its Grand Lodge dues on or before the first day of January, in any year, shall not be represented in the Grand Lodge for that year, except on special permission of the Grand Lodge.

33. *Resolved,* That the lodges with their returns shall send to the Grand Secretary the name of any

representative who may be elected, and the Grand Secretary shall make out a list or roll of representatives from such returns, and if upon calling the roll a quorum of representatives appear to be present, the Grand Lodge shall proceed to business without further delay.

34. *Resolved,* That the accusations or charges against members of lodges or against subordinate lodges, cannot be received from non-affiliated Masons, except in case of charges against a member of a lodge by leave granted by a vote of such lodge, and in case of charges against a subordinate lodge, by leave of the Grand Lodge.

35. *Resolved,* That the R. W. Grand Secretary be directed to have a sufficient number of copies of the Burial Service printed in the same form as the Constitution, and that they be supplied to lodges and members at the cost of publication, and that R. W. Bro. James Fenton be requested to insert the Ritual in his forthcoming new edition of Webb's *Monitor.*

36. *Resolved,* That all members in the jurisdiction of this Grand Lodge be and are hereby interdicted and prohibited from forming incorporate bodies under the laws of this State.

37. *Resolved,* That Sec. 6 of Art. V. of the Constitution does not permit a lodge to recommend the initiation of a rejected candidate in another jurisdiction, but only permits a lodge to reject such candi-

date to another lodge having concurrent or the same jurisdiction.

38. *Resolved,* That it shall not be competent for any subordinate lodge to vote or levy any tax or assessment upon its members for the purchase of real estate, or for the purchasing or building of any Masonic temple or edifice, or for the discharge of any indebtedness incurred for either of said objects.

39. *Resolved,* That in cities or towns where more than one lodge exists, the M. W. G. Master be requested to require the recommendation of a majority of such lodges before issuing a dispensation for a new lodge.

40. *Resolved,* That this Grand Lodge in heretofore or hereafter granting Charters to lodges of brethren of German or foreign nativity or language, does not assent to any change in or modification of the work or lectures, and requires all records, reports and returns to be in English, and that the Worshipful Masters and Wardens shall be familiar with, and well skilled in the work and lectures in the English language.

41. It is not proper for a committee appointed by the Worshipful Master of a lodge to take testimony in a trial of a brother before such lodge, to report the opinion of such committee upon the guilt or innocence of the accused; but they should report the testimony taken by them for the action of the lodge. (Rep. of Com. on Masonic Law, 1869, adopted by G. L.)

42. A Mason indefinitely suspended should apply by petition, which need not be referred. The ballot should be secret. (Rep. of Com. on Gr., 1868, adopted by G. L.)

43. *Resolved,* That any physical injury or imperfection which would render the conferring of any of the degrees upon a candidate, or brother desiring advancement, as required by the work or ritual, either impossible, imperfect or incomplete, is an insuperable objection to further progress, until such injury or imperfection be cured or removed; and, in case of loss of hand or foot, such defect is remediless. (1869.)

CONSTITUTION

OF THE

GRAND LODGE OF MICHIGAN,

Adopted January 11, 1866.

ARTICLE I.

OF THE ORGANIZATION OF THE GRAND LODGE.

SEC. 1. The style of this Grand Lodge shall be "THE GRAND LODGE OF FREE AND ACCEPTED MASONS OF THE STATE OF MICHIGAN."

SEC. 2. The members of the Grand Lodge are, the Grand Officers, Past Grand Masters who are members of subordinate lodges, the W. Masters of chartered lodges, or such representatives as may occasionally be appointed in the room of Masters unable to attend. All Past Masters of subordinate lodges, who are in good standing, are honorary members of the Grand Lodge, without the right to vote.

SEC. 3. The Grand Lodge shall not be opened for work, unless there be present a representation from at least twenty-five subordinate working lodges.

SEC. 4. The annual meetings of the Grand Lodge shall be held on the second Wednesday in January, in such place as may be determined at the Grand Annual Communication, at which meeting the Grand Officers shall be installed. And special meetings may be called by the Grand Master, but no regulation, affecting the general interests of the Craft, shall be changed except at the annual meeting; or special meeting, of which notice of at least one month shall be given to all subordinate lodges.

SEC. 5. The officers of the Grand Lodge are: The Grand Master, Deputy Grand Master, Senior and Junior Grand Wardens, Grand Chaplain, Grand Treasurer, Grand Secretary, Grand Visitor and Lecturer, Grand Architect, Senior and Junior Grand Deacons, Grand Marshal, Grand Sword Bearer, Grand Pursuivant, and Grand Steward and Tiler.

SEC. 6. The Grand Officers shall be titled and rank in the following order, to wit:

1. The Most Worshipful Grand Master.
2. The Rt. Worshipful Deputy Grand Master.
3. The Rt. Worshipful Senior Grand Warden.
4. The Rt. Worshipful Junior Grand Warden.
5. The Most Reverend Grand Chaplain.
6. The R. W. Grand Treasurer.
7. The R. W. Grand Secretary.
8. The R. W. Grand Visitor and Lecturer.

9. The W. Grand Architect.
10. The W. Senior Grand Deacon.
11. The W. Junior Grand Deacon.
12. The Grand Marshal.
13. The Grand Sword Bearer.
14. The Grand Pursuivant.
15. The Grand Steward and Tiler.

ARTICLE II.

OF REPRESENTATIVES TO THE GRAND LODGE.

SEC. 1. Every Brother deputed to represent a Master, in case he is absent, shall be furnished with a certificate of his appointment, under the seal of the lodge appointing him, and the attestation of the Secretary thereof.

SEC. 2. Representatives of Masters shall be chosen from among the members of the lodge appointing them; except, that lodges in the Upper Peninsula, (so called,) of this jurisdiction, shall have the right to be represented by proxies to brethren, duly certified as in Sec. 1, not members of their respective lodges: *Provided,* Such persons shall be members of some lodge in this jurisdiction.

SEC. 3. No Master, or representative from any subordinate lodge shall be permitted to sit in that capacity in the Grand Lodge, at the Annual Grand Communication, until all the dues from such lodge, to the Grand Lodge, are paid: *Provided,* That a Grand Lodge can be otherwise formed.

ARTICLE III.

OF ELECTIONS.

SEC. 1. The M. W. Grand Master, R. W. Deputy Grand Master, R. W. Senior and Junior Grand Wardens, the R. W. Grand Treasurer, the R. W. Grand Secretary and the R. W. Grand Visitor and Lecturer shall be elected by ballot, or otherwise, as the Grand Lodge may, from time to time, determine, and shall hold their offices for one year, and until their successors are elected and installed. A majority of all the votes shall be necessary to a choice in each case above enumerated. All other officers shall be appointed by the Grand Master elect for his term.

SEC. 2. Each Grand Officer shall be, and continue, a working member of a subordinate lodge, but not eligible to an office of a higher grade than he may have attained in his said lodge.

SEC. 3. Each member of the Grand Lodge, representing a subordinate lodge, shall be entitled to three votes, and other regular members of the Grand Lodge to one vote.

SEC. 4. A Worshipful Master, or representative of a lodge U. D., is not privileged to vote in the Grand Lodge, until the said lodge is chartered, and he duly installed. He may be allowed to speak to all questions, and shall be entitled to the same mileage and per diem attendance as members.

ARTICLE IV.

OF THE POWERS AND DUTIES OF THE OFFICERS OF THE GRAND LODGE.

SEC. 1. The M. W. Grand Master has authority to convene the Grand Lodge whenever it shall appear to him that the interests of the Craft render the same necessary or expedient, and in case of the death or removal of a Grand Officer, or the refusal of any Grand Officer elect to serve or be personally installed therein, and in all cases of vacancy he shall have power to fill such vacancy by the nomination, appointment, and installation of any Brother otherwise eligible to the same. He is invested with the power of granting dispensations at his discretion, during the recess of the Grand Lodge; to convene any subordinate lodge at his pleasure; preside therein; inspect the proceedings of the same, and to require a strict conformity to the rules of the fraternity; but he is prohibited from making Masons at sight. He may appoint a District Deputy Grand Master for the Upper Peninsula, with like powers, to hold his office at the pleasure of the Grand Master and subject to his orders at all times.

SEC. 2. In case of the death or absence of the M. W. Grand Master, the R. W. Deputy Grand Master shall preside at the meetings of the Grand Lodge, and shall exercise all the powers, and become liable to perform all the duties of the M. W. Grand Master.

SEC. 3. The R. W. Grand Wardens, in case of the

death or absence of the M. W. Grand Master and R. W. Deputy Grand Master shall, according to seniority, preside at the meeting of the Grand Lodge, and assume the prerogatives and duties of Grand Master, for all regular and necessary purposes. They shall assist in the administration of the affairs of the Grand Lodge, and diligently preserve and maintain the ancient landmarks of the Order, throughout the jurisdiction.

SEC. 4. The R. W. Grand Treasurer shall keep a just and fair account of all moneys received and paid by him on account of the Grand Lodge, and shall exhibit a statement of such receipts and payments at its annual meeting. He shall promptly pay the drafts of the presiding officer of the Grand Lodge, attested by the R. W. Grand Secretary, out of any moneys in his hands belonging to the Grand Lodge, and shall be required by the Grand Master to give security for the faithful performance of his trust.

SEC. 5. It is made the duty of the R. W. Grand Secretary to record the transactions of the Grand Lodge; to register all warrants, dispensations, certificates, and the names of all the members of subordinate lodges returned for registry; to furnish the chairman of every committee with the files, records and papers in his custody relating to the business of such committee; to receive, file and record all petitions, applications and appeals, and sign and certify all instruments issued by authority of the Grand Lodge; to receive, credit and record all moneys paid into the Grand Lodge, and pay over the same without delay to the R. W. Grand Treasurer. He is charged with all the correspondence of the Grand Lodge, under direction of the M. W. Grand Master, and, in conformity with the established usages of Masonry, he shall attend upon the Grand Lodge or the M. W. Grand Master, when required, with all records and papers that may be necessary for the transaction of business. He shall keep an account of all penalties incurred, and report the same to the Grand Lodge. He shall countersign all drafts upon the R. W. Grand Treasurer; keep an accurate account with the several Lodges under this jurisdiction; have charge of the seal; issue summons when directed by the senior officer of the Grand Lodge; countersign, when required, all diplomas granted by subordinate lodges, and certify to the regularity and good standing of such lodge, and shall affix thereto the seal of this Grand Lodge, and shall be entitled to receive for the same the sum of fifty cents. He shall give early notice to the Grand Lodges in correspondence with this Grand Lodge, of any changes which may take place in its officers, accompanied with specimens of their handwriting and true signatures, and shall, at the same time, request a reciprocation of similar documents, and shall do and perform all such duties as are incidental to his office, and incumbent on him by general usage; and shall receive such compensation as the Grand Lodge may direct.

SEC. 6. The M. Rev. Grand Chaplain shall perform the religious services and solemnities of the Grand Lodge.

SEC. 7. The W. Grand Deacons shall perform their proper Masonic duties, and assist within the body of the Grand Lodge.

SEC. 8. The R. W. Grand Visitor and Lecturer shall perform such duties as may be required of him by the M. W. Grand Master or the Grand Lodge, but shall be entitled to no compensation, or to lecture in any lodge, without a certificate from the M. W. Grand Master and R. W. Grand Secretary that they have examined him in the lectures and find him fully competent to instruct.

SEC. 9. The W. Grand Architect shall attend and officiate at the laying of corner stones of public edifices, and on other occasions when required.

SEC. 10. The Grand Marshal shall proclaim the Grand Officers at their installations, conduct all the processions of the Grand Lodge or the Grand Master.

SEC. 11. The Grand Sword Bearer shall carry the sword in procession, and perform such other duties as pertain to his office.

SEC. 12. The Grand Stewards shall provide suitable refreshments when directed so to do by the Grand Lodge, and shall superintend the provision to be made for festivals.

SEC. 13. The Grand Pursuivant shall communicate with the Grand Tiler; announce in due Masonic form all applications for admission; and have in charge the jewels and regalia of the Grand Lodge.

SEC. 14. The Grand Tiler shall guard the door of the Grand Lodge on the outside, report all persons claiming admission, and see that none enter unauthorized. He shall summon the Grand Lodge when required, and discharge such other official duties as it may, from time to time, direct, for which service he shall be entitled to an equitable compensation from the Grand Lodge. He shall have no vote therein during his continuance in office: and no brother below the degree of Master Mason shall be eligible to the office.

ARTICLE V.

OF SUBORDINATE LODGES.

SEC. 1. No subordinate lodge under this jurisdiction shall hold more than one regular meeting in each lunar month, except the festivals of St. John's. No lodge shall hold any meeting on the Holy Sabbath, except on funeral occasions or in cases of charity.

SEC. 2. A subordinate lodge shall consist of a Master, Senior and Junior Wardens, Treasurer, Secretary, Senior and Junior Deacons, Tiler, and as many members as may be convenient: and shall have a seal.

SEC. 3. No brother shall be eligible to the office of Master of a lodge, unless he shall previously have been a Warden of a regular lodge; except in case of the formation of a new lodge.

SEC. 4. The Master and the Senior and Junior Wardens shall be annually elected by ballot at the regular communication of the lodge next preceding the festival of St. John the Evangelist, unless otherwise ordered by the Grand Lodge, or M. W. Grand Master during vacation: except in the Upper Peninsula, where they may be elected at the first regular meeting in November. They shall hold their offices for one year, and until others are elected and installed in their stead. Each member of the lodge in good standing, shall be entitled to one vote, and in case of a tie, the presiding officer shall have an additional vote. All the other officers of the lodge shall be elected or appointed in such manner as each lodge may determine.

SEC. 5. By the term jurisdiction is understood the geographical center between contiguous lodges, except in cities or villages, lodges in which shall have concurrent jurisdiction, and the same shall extend to at least the limits of such city or village.

SEC. 6. No lodge shall initiate a candidate who does not reside, and has not resided six months within the jurisdiction of said lodge, or who has been, within one year previously, rejected by another lodge, unless recommended by vote of the lodge in which he was rejected, or from whose jurisdiction he shall hail.

SEC. 7. It shall be the duty of each lodge under this jurisdiction, to communicate all rejections to contiguous lodges as well as to the Grand Lodge, accurate records of which shall be kept by each lodge.

transmitting the same, and no application for initiation shall be renewed in any lodge within two months after rejection.

SEC. 8. No candidate for initiation can withdraw his petition after the same has been referred to a committee, without the concurrence of two-thirds of the members present.

SEC. 9. Every candidate for advancement in any lodge under this jurisdiction, shall first be examined in open lodge and demonstrate his proficiency in the degree or degrees previously conferred.

SEC. 10. No lodge under this jurisdiction shall confer the degrees of Entered Apprentice, Fellow Craft and Master Mason, (unless the candidate be a clergyman,) for any less sum than twenty-one dollars, and the fees for each degree shall be paid in cash at or before the time of receiving the same. No credit shall be allowed.

SEC. 11. It shall be the duty of the Secretary of each lodge (in addition to his other duties) to transmit to the R. W. Grand Secretary at least two weeks before the annual meeting of the Grand Lodge in each year, a return of the officers and members of his lodge, and also of all resignations, withdrawals or deaths which may have taken place since the preceding return, in conformity with the forms hereto annexed, and keep on file a duplicate thereof.

SEC. 12. No Mason can be a member of more than one lodge at the same time; nor shall any member be permitted to withdraw from his lodge until all his dues to the same are paid or remitted.

SEC. 13. No voluntarily unaffiliated Mason residing within the accredited jurisdiction of a working lodge shall visit the same more than three times. Subordinate lodges have disciplinary control over non-affiliated Masons residing within their respective jurisdictions.

ARTICLE VI.

MISCELLANEOUS REGULATIONS.

SEC. 1. No Entered Apprentice or Fellow Craft, initiated or passed in any lodge within this jurisdiction shall, without the consent of the same, be passed or received into any other lodge than that in which he was so initiated or passed.

SEC. 2. No candidate for initiation or membership shall be proposed or balloted for at any other than a regular communication; nor shall such proposition and ballot be had at one and the same communication. No ballot for degrees shall be had in any but a Master's lodge, and not for more than one degree at a time. For initiation or advancement, one black ball rejects; for membership, three, but the ballot may pass a second time only, to avoid mistakes.

SEC. 3. None but Master Masons can be members of a lodge.

SEC. 4. Each subordinate lodge shall have power to hear and determine on matters of difference between its own members, and suspend or expel with the concurrence of two-thirds of the members present. In case of suspension two-thirds of the members may restore, but in one of expulsion an unanimous vote shall be required.

SEC. 5. Any brother deeming himself aggrieved by the decision of his lodge, may appeal, in writing, to the Grand Lodge, by whom such order shall be taken relating thereto, as the nature of the case may require.

SEC. 6. Every lodge within this jurisdiction shall have and enjoy full power to regulate its internal police by the adoption of a constitution, by-laws, and other regulations, not inconsistent with the provisions of this constitution, or the ancient usages of the fraternity.

SEC. 7. No lodge can surrender its charter to the Grand Lodge without first taking the same steps at a regular meeting thereof, which, by its constitution or by-laws would have been required for amendments to said instrument, or for its total abrogation; and in all cases, written notice of the intention to surrender a charter shall be given to every member of said lodge, within its jurisdiction, at least one month preceding the regular meeting at which action is proposed to be had.

SEC. 8. Lodges are required upon the expulsion of a brother for any other cause than non-payment of dues, forthwith to make a report of their proceedings in the case, to the R. W. Grand Secretary, in order that, in the event of an appeal, the Grand Lodge may be enabled to come to an immediate decision thereon.

SEC. 9. Any lodge neglecting to assemble for one year, or to make returns and pay its dues for two years, shall forfeit its warrant and surrender the same to the R. W. Grand Secretary.

SEC. 10. There shall be no funeral or other procession of Masons under this jurisdiction, except by permission of a regularly constituted lodge, or of the presiding officer thereof.

SEC. 11. The revenues of this Grand Lodge shall be derived from the following sources, to wit:

For every warrant to form a new lodge,......	$100 00
For every dispensation to form a new lodge, (to be applied as part of the fees for a warrant, in case the lodge shall be subsequently warranted by the Grand Lodge,)........	50 00
For a dispensation to confer degrees—for each degree	5 00
For every Grand Lodge certificate, including Secretary's fees, and exclusive of cost of blanks, ...	1 00
For every person initiated,......................	1 00
For every Master Mason from without the jurisdiction of this Grand Lodge admitted as a member of a lodge within the same,..	1 00
Subordinate lodges shall pay annually for each of its members of three months' standing or over, (honorary members, Secretaries and suspended members excepted).....	25

SEC. 12. It shall be the duty of the Committee of Accounts to report to the Grand Lodge annually the state of its funds.

Sec. 13. It shall be the duty of all lodges under this jurisdiction to be particularly careful to admit no candidate of bad moral character or intemperate habits within their lodges, and whenever that vice shall appear among their own members, it shall be the duty of the lodge, forthwith, to appoint a suitable committee to wait upon such brother and forewarn him or them of the evil consequences, and if not reclaimed, after a reasonable time, such lodge or lodges shall forthwith proceed to make out a summons for such offenders, to appear before the lodge to answer for such un-masonic conduct, and unless such offender shall satisfy the lodge that he will abandon such habits, (and in that case they may stay further proceedings until sufficient opportunity be given to test the sincerity of the promise,) they shall proceed to suspend him for a limited time, and when that shall have expired, if not reclaimed, then they shall proceed to expel him from all the benefits of Masonry.

Sec. 14. The use of distilled spirits or fermented drinks in lodge rooms, at lodge meetings, is of evil example and productive of pernicious effects. The same is therefore expressly and absolutely forbidden under any pretence whatever.

Sec. 15. This Grand Lodge shall have, exercise and enjoy, full and complete appellate and corrective powers, in all cases relative to the fraternity, within the State of Michigan. It shall have power to assess such contributions, from time to time, as the welfare of the Craft may require, and to warrant and organize lodges within this State. All warrants for lodges shall be prepared by the R. W. Grand Secretary and signed by the Grand Officers.

Sec. 16. No lodge or assembly of Master Masons which shall hereafter be formed within the State of Michigan, shall be deemed legal without the sanction of this Grand Lodge being first obtained. Masonic communication, either public or private, between lodges and their members, under this jurisdiction, and such illegal lodge or assembly, and any member or members thereof, is strictly forbidden, under the penalty of expulsion from the benefits of Masonry.

Sec. 17. This Grand Lodge adopts the work approved and recommended by the National Convention of Grand Lodges held at Baltimore, Md., in May, A. L. 5843, being the same which was re-affirmed by this Grand Lodge at its session in 1865.

Sec. 18. All amendments and additions to this Constitution must be submitted and approved at a previous meeting to that in which they are acted upon; or a copy of such alteration, addition or amendment must be forwarded to the Master of each of the lodges under this jurisdiction, at least two months previous to being acted upon.

Sec. 19. This Constitution, except the election and installation of officers, shall take effect at the close of the present session, and as to such election it takes immediate effect.

REVISED BY-LAWS

OF THE

GRAND LODGE OF MICHIGAN.

Art. 1. At every communication of this Grand Lodge previous to the transaction of business, the lodge shall be opened in proper form.

Art. 2. The lodge to be opened within half an hour of the time appointed in the Constitution, or in the notification in the case of an extra meeting, or as soon thereafter as a sufficient number shall appear.

Art. 3. No person shall be admitted in the Grand Lodge before his name shall be announced and leave given by the presiding officer; nor shall any brother be admitted into the Grand Lodge but such as are members, representatives, or members of a subordinate lodge, or admitted as a witness, petitioner, or by a vote of this Grand Lodge.

Art. 4. After reading the proceedings of the last meeting, the appointment of committees shall be first in order; then the presenting and hearing petitions; the reports of committees previously appointed, and the unfinished business; and no new motion or other business shall be received without first obtaining leave of the Grand Lodge, until the former is disposed of.

ART. 5. The committees to be appointed at each stated meeting of the Grand Lodge, in pursuance of the preceding article, are:

A Committee on Masonic Law,
A Committee on Grievances,
A Committee on Accounts,
A Committee on Examination, and
A Committee on Foreign Correspondence,
} To consist of three members each.

The first four to report before closing the lodge, and the latter at the next regular meeting of the Grand Lodge; to which, in the meantime, the R. W. Grand Secretary shall transmit the proceedings and other communications received from the several Grand Lodges in correspondence with this Grand Lodge.

ART. 6. All committees shall be appointed by the M. W. Grand Master, unless otherwise specially directed by the Grand Lodge. In case of a ballot, a majority of votes shall be necessary to a choice.

ART. 7. When a member is about to speak, he shall rise from his seat, and respectfully address himself to the "Most Worshipful Grand Master."

ART. 8. If a member, in speaking or otherwise, shall transgress the rules of the Grand Lodge, any member may call him to order, and he shall immediately sit down, unless permitted to explain. The M. W. Grand Master shall decide all questions of order, without debate, with the right of appeal from his decision to the Grand Lodge, in all cases where the imperative charges assented to by the M. W. Grand Master at his installation are not thereby infringed. And any member called to order may be either permitted to proceed, or shall be censured, or fined, as may be determined upon.

Art. 9. No motion for reconsideration shall be in order, unless made within twenty-four hours after the question shall have been decided; nor shall it be in order unless moved by one of the majority.

Art. 10. No member or Lodge shall vote on any question in the event of which he or it is immediately interested; nor shall any member vote if he was not present when the question was stated.

Art. 11. Every motion requiring to be recorded, shall be in writing.

Art. 12. When a motion is made and seconded, it shall be stated by the presiding officer, or read by the R. W. Grand Secretary, if in writing, and the question of consideration shall then first be decided.

Art. 13. When the reading of any paper is called for and objected to by a member, it shall be determined by vote.

Art. 14. No new motion or proposition, except to call off or to close, shall be admitted while a question is pending before the Grand Lodge.

Art. 15. No person shall speak more than twice on any one subject, unless he obtain the consent of the Grand Lodge.

Art. 16. All reports of committees shall be made

in writing, and signed by at least a majority of the committee.

ART. 17. Any of the above By-Laws may be amended, or, when necessary, postponed for the time being, on the concurrence of two-thirds of the members present, or a majority of the lodges.

ART. 18. The usual rules of parliamentary practice governing American legislative bodies are not objectionable in Grand or subordinate lodges, so far as they do not conflict with the peculiarities of the Masonic Institution, or with the well known prerogatives of its officers.

ART. 19. The election and installation of officers of the Grand Lodge shall be the last order of business of the session.

ART. 20. Under the direction of the Grand Marshal, seats for the members of the Grand Lodge shall be reserved in the East; and all visiting brethren be requested to sit in the West, at all future communications of this Grand Lodge.

ROLL OF OFFICERS

OF THE

GRAND LODGE OF MICHIGAN.

Historical Note.—The Grand Lodge of Michigan has existed under two distinct and successive organizations. The first organization was formed at a convention held in the city of Detroit, on the 24th of June, 1826, at which the following representatives were present, viz: Henry J. Hunt, John L. Whitney and Austin E. Wing, from Zion Lodge, No. 3; John Garrison and Charles Jackson, from Detroit Lodge, No. 337; Andrew J. Whitney and Marshall Chapin, proxies for Menominee Lodge, No. 374, and John Anderson, from Monroe Lodge, No. 375. A constitution was adopted, and an election ordered for the 31st of July following; upon which date the first grand officers were elected, with Hon. Lewis Cass as Grand Master. By the constitution the annual election of officers took place in June; and in June,

1827, we accordingly find Hon. Lewis Cass again elected Grand Master. The names of his subordinates for both years appear in order in the subjoined roll. On the 8th and 9th of August following, special communications were held, but the record says, "a quorum not appearing, no business was transacted." Here began the *days of darkness*, when the fell spirit of proscription and persecution was rampant; and no further communication was held, nor action taken, for almost fourteen years. This was the Masonic interregnum, of which the fathers tell us. Stony Creek Lodge, in Oakland County, was the only lodge in Michigan that continued in successful working during this period.

On the 2d of June, 1841, the Grand Lodge again assembled, rebuilt its fallen altars, and started upon a new career. At this communication Levi Cook was elected Grand Master. From this point the business of the Grand Lodge went forward in the usual order until the 22d of May, 1844, when it was "*Resolved*, That in view of the difficulties with the Grand Lodge of New York in acknowledging the authority of this Grand Lodge, it be recommended to the members of the old lodges of this State, holding their charters from the Grand Lodge of New York, to apply to that body for a renewal of their charters for the purpose of immediate reorganization; and that in case the renewal of these lodges be granted under the above authority, and upon the above conditions, this Grand Lodge does hereby recommend said lodges to take immediate steps for forming a Grand Lodge, and that as soon as said Grand Lodge shall have been so organized, this Grand Lodge shall be dissolved." The old lodges having obtained new charters in pursuance of the above recommendation, a convention was held at Detroit, on the 17th of September, 1844, at which the present Grand Lodge was organized; John Mullett being elected as the first Grand Master. By the new constitution the annual communication and election of officers were made to occur in January, at which date they have ever since stood.

The fact of the last annual election under the old organization being held in June, 1844, and the first election of officers under the new organization being held in September, of the same year, explains the repetition of the names of officers for that year.

The present Grand Lodge was incorporated by act of the Legislature in 1849, which act was amended in 1869. (Laws of 1849, page 313; Laws of 1869, page 115.)

Since the new organization no material changes have taken place. The harmony and prosperity of the order have been uninterrupted, of which fact the official roll constitutes in itself one of the strongest and most interesting proofs.

In the preparation of this roll the utmost care has been taken to render it correct. The ancient records have been carefully consulted, in which regard most material and generous aid has been given by our present Grand Secretary, Bro. James Fenton. The compiler does not assume that it is absolutely without defect, but he assures his brethren that he has made it as nearly perfect as it was possible for him to do, and that it has been prepared with the express intention of making it a reliable standard of reference.

It has been prepared, not merely for its utility, but also as a deserved tribute to the memory of those illustrious craftsmen whose names are here enrolled; names some of which stand emblazoned upon our nation's escutcheon, an honor alike to Masonry, to civilization and to humanity.

M. W. GRAND MASTERS.

OLD ORGANIZATION, JUNE 24TH, 1826.

Hon. Lewis Cass........ 1826-27

(*Interregnum*,)

Levi Cook........ 1841
Leonard Weed........ 1842
John Mullett........ 1843-44

NEW ORGANIZATION, SEPTEMBER 17TH, 1844.

John Mullett........ 1844-45
Ebenezer Hall........ 1846
E. Smith Lee........ 1847-48
Jeremiah Moors........ 1849-50
Henry T. Backus........ 1851-52-53
George W. Peck........ 1854-55
George C. Munro........ 1856
Levi Cook........ 1857
William M. Fenton........ 1858
J. Adams Allen........ 1859
William L. Greenly........ 1860
Horace S. Roberts........ 1861

Francis Darrow.. 1862
J. Eastman Johnson.. 1863
Lovell Moore.. 1864
William T. Mitchell.. 1865
Salathiel C. Coffinbury.. 1866-67-68
Abraham T. Metcalf.. 1869

R. W. DEPUTY GRAND MASTERS.

OLD ORGANIZATION.

Andrew J. Whitney.. 1826
James Abbot.. 1827

(*Interregnum.*)

Leonard Weed.. 1841
John E. Schwarz.. 1842
Ebenezer Hall.. 1843-44

NEW ORGANIZATION.

J. D. Dutton.. 1844
Ebenezer Hall.. 1845
Jacob Beeson.. 1846-47
Paul B. Ring.. 1848-49
John Barber.. 1850
John Stewart.. 1851
Alfred Treadway.. 1852
James A. Hahn.. 1853
George C. Munro.. 1854-55
Horace S. Roberts.. 1856
T. H. Lyon.. 1857
J. Adams Allen.. 1858
William L. Greenly.. 1859
Simeon B. Brown.. 1860
Francis Darrow.. 1861
J. Eastman Johnson.. 1862
Lovell Moore.. 1863
William T. Mitchell.. 1864
Salathiel C. Coffinbury.. 1865
Abraham T. Metcalf.. 1866-67-68
Alanson Partridge.. 1869

R. W. DISTRICT DEPUTY GRAND MASTERS FOR UPPER PENINSULA.

Thomas U. Flanner.. 1866-67-68
Thomas N. Lee.. 1869

R. W. SENIOR GRAND WARDENS.

OLD ORGANIZATION.

Seneca Allen... 1826-27

(Interregnum.)

Martin Davis.. 1841
Ebenezer Hall.. 1842
William Jones.. 1843
John Farrar 1844

NEW ORGANIZATION.

Calvin Hotchkiss.. 1844-45-46
Paul B. Ring.. 1847
Joshua B. Taylor.. 1848
John Stewart.. 1849-50
Wm. H. McOmber.. 1851
James A. Hahn.. 1852
George C. Munro... 1853
Horace S. Roberts.. 1854-55
Willys C. Ransom.. 1856
Jas. C. Wood.. 1857
H. T. Farnum.. 1858
H. C. Hodge.. 1859
David A. Wright... 1860
F. Carlisle.. 1861-62
Michael Ayers... 1863
Abraham T. Metcalf.. 1864-65
Alanson Partridge... 1866-67-68
Edwin R. Landon... 1869

R. W. JUNIOR GRAND WARDENS.

OLD ORGANIZATION.

Leonard Weed........ 1826
Martin Davis........ 1827

(*Interregnum.*)

Ebenezer Hall........ 1841
William Jones........ 1842
Joshua B. Taylor........ 1843
Peleg Ewell........ 1844

NEW ORGANIZATION.

John E. Schwarz........ 1844
Joshua B. Taylor........ 1845-46-47
John Stewart........ 1848
Wm. H. McOmber........ 1849-50
Alfred Treadway........ 1851
George C. Munro........ 1852
George W. Wilson........ 1853
Warren P. Mills........ 1854-55
John B. Hamilton........ 1856-57
B. B. Church........ 1858
David A. Wright........ 1859
Elisha Leach........ 1860
Palmer H. Taylor........ 1861
Michael Ayers........ 1862
Abraham T. Metcalf........ 1863
Alanson Partridge........ 1864-65
David A. Wright........ 1866-67
Edwin R. Landon........ 1868
John V. Lambertson........ 1869

M. REV. GRAND CHAPLAINS.

OLD ORGANIZATION.

Smith Weeks........ 1826-27

(Interregnum.)

Samuel Silsby........ 1841–42
A. S. Wells........ 1843
O. C. Comstock........ 1844

NEW ORGANIZATION.

Daniel Michael........ 1845–46–47
E. M. Crippen........ 1848–49–50
Sidney S. Brown........ 1851–52
Daniel C. Jacokes........ 1853–54
Sidney S. Brown........ 1855–56
Levi H. Corson........ 1857
Benj. F. Doughty........ 1858
Israel Cogshall........ 1859
George Taylor........ 1860–61–62
Daniel B. Tracy........ 1863–64
Samuel Clements, Jr........ 1865
Daniel B. Tracy........ 1866
George Taylor........ 1867
I. Boynton........ 1868
C. C. Yemans........ 1969

R. W. GRAND TREASURERS.

OLD ORGANIZATION.

Henry J. Hunt........ 1826
Philip Lecuyer........ 1827

(Interregnum.)

Calvin Hotchkiss........ 1841 to 1844

NEW ORGANIZATION.

Charles Jackson........ 1844
Levi Cook........ 1845 to 1852
Wm. H. McOmber........ 1853 to 1862
Rufus W. Landon........ 1863 to 1869

R. W. GRAND SECRETARIES.

OLD ORGANIZATION.

John L. Whitney	1826-27

(Interregnum.)

Abner C. Smith	1841 to 1844

NEW ORGANIZATION.

E. Smith Lee	1844-45-46
Abner C. Smith	1847
James Fenton	1848 to 1869

R. W. GRAND VISITOR AND LECTURERS.

OLD ORGANIZATION.

Peleg Ewell	1842
Abner C. Smith	1843
Jeremiah Moors	1844

NEW ORGANIZATION.

J. D. Dutton	1846
William S. Brown	1847
Abner C. Smith	1848-49-50
George F. Gardner	1851
E. Smith Lee	1852
Benjamin Porter Jr	1853
Bela Cogshall	1854-55-56
Stillman Blanchard	1857 to 1868
Henry M. Look	1869

W. GRAND ARCHITECTS.

Albert H. Jordan	1860-61
William Barclay	1862-63-64
Reuben Bulman	1865-66

James W. Gilbert 1867-68
Reuben Bulman 1869

W. SENIOR GRAND DEACONS.

OLD ORGANIZATION.

Moses Conn 1842
Charles Jackson 1843
Moses Conn 1844

NEW ORGANIZATION.

John Farrar 1845-46
Madison Cook 1847
Thomas Cook 1848
G. W. Thomas 1849-50
John Clancey 1851
William L. Greenly 1852
Horace S. Roberts 1853
Willys C. Ransom 1854-55
Rufus W. Landon 1856-57
E. A. Brown 1858
Elisha Leach 1859
F. Carlisle 1860
Michael Ayers 1861
George W. Wilson 1862
Sardis F. Hubbell 1863
David A. Wright 1864-65
J. F. Lowry 1866
Edwin R. Landon 1867
Joseph B. Bampton 1868
Carlos G. Curtis 1869

W. JUNIOR GRAND DEACONS.

OLD ORGANIZATION.

Joshua B. Taylor 1842
J. D. Davis 1843
H. N. Church 1844

NEW ORGANIZATION.

Moses Conn........ 1845-46
Czar Jones........ 1847
R. B. Loomis........ 1848
Alfred Treadway........ 1849-50
C. F. Loomis........ 1851
J. E. Hoyt........ 1852
Philo Beckwith........ 1853
T. B. Eldred........ 1854-55
Edwin R. Merrifield........ 1856
E. A. Brown........ 1857
Elisha Leach........ 1858
David H. Lord........ 1859
T. H. Tracy........ 1860
R. B. Piper........ 1861
T. H. Tracy........ 1862
Palmer H. Taylor........ 1863
D. H. Baker........ 1864-65
C. J. Kruger........ 1866
P. B. Haight........ 1867
Warren Green........ 1868
Seth Pettibone........ 1869

GRAND MARSHALS.

OLD ORGANIZATION.

S. C. Munson........ 1842
Levi Cook........ 1843-44

NEW ORGANIZATION.

John E. Schwarz........ 1846-47
William S. Brown........ 1848
John E. Schwarz........ 1849
A. P. Hogarth........ 1850
E. Perry........ 1851
Harlehigh Cartter........ 1852
George Hill........ 1853
Joseph P. Whiting........ 1854-55-56
Warren P. Mills........ 1857
Joseph P. Whiting........ 1858 to 1861

J. S. Judson........ 1862
Joseph P. Whiting........ 1863-64
Oliver Dodge........ 1865
N. Buel Eldridge........ 1866
D. R. Stroud........ 1867-68
Frederick Hart........ 1869

GRAND SWORD BEARERS.

OLD ORGANIZATION.

Jacob Loop........ 1842
John S. Park........ 1843
Calvin Chapel........ 1844

NEW ORGANIZATION.

Charles W. Millerd........ 1847
John E. Schwarz........ 1848
R. B. Loomis........ 1849
E. Pratt........ 1850
George W. Wilson........ 1851
Joseph P. Whiting........ 1852
Jesse Button........ 1853
R. B. Piper........ 1854-55
E. A. Brown........ 1856
John R. Baker........ 1857
Warren P. Mills........ 1858-59
T. B. Eldred........ 1860
Alanson Partridge........ 1861
R. B. Piper........ 1862
Oliver Bourke........ 1863
C. J. Kruger........ 1864
George E. Hubbard........ 1865
Arthur M. Clark........ 1866
Andrew J. Cummings........ 1867
George R. Hurd........ 1868
J. L. Mitchell........ 1869

GRAND PURSUIVANTS.

OLD ORGANIZATION.

John E. Schwarz........ 1826-27

(*Interregnum.*)

Jacob Loop.. 1841
John Farrar.. 1842-43
Thomas M. Perry.. 1844

NEW ORGANIZATION.

Jeremiah Moors.. 1846
James Fenton.. 1847
Madison Cook.. 1848
Joseph T. Copeland.. 1849
George C. Munro.. 1850
William L. Greenly.. 1851
Jefferson G. Thurber.. 1852
John R. Baker.. 1853 to 1856
Francis Darrow.. 1857
T. B. Eldred.. 1858
Francis Darrow.. 1859
Alanson Partridge.. 1860
A. Bernard Cudworth.. 1861
E. P. Worden.. 1862
Henry Metz.. 1863-64
L. A. Rogers.. 1865
W. F. King.. 1866
Nathan Manly.. 1867
John L. Newell.. 1868
Willys C. Ransom.. 1869

GRAND STEWARD AND TILERS.

OLD ORGANIZATION.

Samuel Sherwood.. 1826
Daniel P. Colo.. 1827

(*Interregnum.*)

Peleg Ewell.. 1841
Stephen W. Palmer.. 1842
Seneca Caswell.. 1843-44

NEW ORGANIZATION.

Seneca Caswell.. 1844 to 1854
Charles D. Howard.. 1855 to 1865
Wm. V. Griffith.. 1866 to 1869

THE ANCIENT LANDMARKS OF FREEMASONRY.

The Ancient Landmarks of Freemasonry are those universal and immutable laws and regulations which form the basis and distinguishing characteristics of the Order, and which have existed from time immemorial. Their essential elements are antiquity that reaches beyond memory or history, and universal recognition and observance among regular Masons. But their most striking peculiarity is that they are *unrepealable;* and it is beyond the legitimate power of any body of Masons to change or modify them in the slightest particular.

They are either *unwritten* or *written.* The unwritten landmarks are those peculiar marks of distinction by which Masons are separated from the outer world. To this class belong most of the methods of recognition, as also the more material portions of the entire body of esoteric Masonry.

The written landmarks are distinguished by the same characteristics as the unwritten, except that of secrecy; they being public in their nature. They are twenty-five in number, and are classed by the highest authorities in the following order.

Landmark First.

The modes of recognition are, of all the Landmarks, the most legitimate and unquestioned. They admit of no variation; and if ever they have suffered alteration or addition, the evil of such a violation of the ancient law has always made itself subsequently manifest.

Landmark Second.

The division of Symbolic Masonry into three degrees, is a Landmark that has been better preserved than almost any other.

Landmark Third.

The legend of the Third Degree is an important Landmark, the integrity of which has been well preserved. There is no rite of Masonry, practised in any country or language, in which the essential elements of this legend are not taught. The lectures may vary, and indeed are constantly changing, but the legend has ever remained substantially the same. And it is necessary that it should be so, for the legend of the Temple Builder constitutes the very essence and identity of Masonry. Any rite which should exclude it, or materially alter it, would at once, by that exclusion or alteration, cease to be a Masonic rite.

Landmark Fourth.

The government of the Fraternity, by a presiding officer called a *Grand Master*, who is elected from the body of the craft, is a fourth Landmark of the Order. Many persons ignorantly suppose that the election of the Grand Master is held in consequence of a law or regulation of the Grand Lodge. Such, however, is not the case. The office is indebted for its existence to a Landmark of the Order. Grand Masters are to be found in the records of the institution long before Grand Lodges were established; and if the present system of legislative government by Grand Lodges were to be abolished, a Grand Master would still be necessary. In fact, although there has been a period within the records of history, and indeed of very recent date, when a Grand Lodge was unknown, there never has been a time when the craft did not have their Grand Master.

Landmark Fifth.

The prerogative of the Grand Master to preside over every assembly of the craft, wheresoever and whensoever held, is a fifth Landmark. It is in consequence of this law, derived from ancient usage, and not from any special enactment, that the Grand Master assumes the chair, or as it is called in England, "the throne," at every communication of the Grand Lodge; and that he is also entitled to preside at the communication of every subordinate lodge, where he may happen to be present.

Landmark Sixth.

The prerogative of the Grand Master to grant dispensations for conferring degrees at irregular times, is another and very important Landmark. The statutory law of Masonry requires a month, or other determinate period, to elapse between the presentation of a petition and the election of a candidate. But the Grand Master has the power to set aside or dispense with this probation, and to allow a candidate to be initiated at once.

Landmark Seventh.

The prerogative of the Grand Master to give dispensations for opening and holding lodges, is another Landmark. He may grant, in virtue of this, to a sufficient number of Masons, the privilege of meeting together and conferring degrees. The lodges thus established are called "Lodges under Dispensation." They are strictly creatures of the Grand Master, created by his authority, existing only during his will and pleasure, and liable at any moment to be dissolved at his command. They may be continued for a day, a month, or six months; but whatever be the period of their existence, they are indebted for that existence solely to the grace of the Grand Master.

Landmark Eighth.

The prerogative of the Grand Master to make Masons at sight, is a Landmark which is closely connected with the preceding one. There has been much misapprehension in relation to this Landmark, which misapprehension has sometimes led to a denial of its existence in jurisdictions where the Grand Master was perhaps at the very time substantially exercising the prerogative, without the slightest remark or opposition. It is not to be supposed that the Grand Master can retire with a profane into a private room, and there, without assistance, confer the degrees of Freemasonry upon him. No such prerogative exists, and yet many believe that this is the so much talked of right of "making Masons at sight." The real mode, and the only mode of exercising the prerogative is this: The Grand Master summons to his assistance not less than six other Masons, convenes a lodge, and without any previous probation, but *on sight* of the candidate, confers the degrees upon him, after which he dissolves the lodge, and dismisses the brethren. Lodges thus convened for special purposes are called "occasional lodges." The making of Masons at sight is only the conferring of the degrees by the Grand Master, at once, in an occasional lodge, constituted by his dispensing power for the purpose, and over which he presides in person.

Landmark Ninth.

The necessity for Masons to congregate in lodges is another Landmark. It is not to be understood by this that any ancient Landmark has directed that permanent organization of subordinate lodges which constitutes one of the features of the Masonic system as it now prevails. But the Landmarks of the Order always prescribed that Masons should from time to time congregate together, for the purpose of either operative or speculative labor, and that these congregations should be called *Lodges.*

Landmark Tenth.

The government of the Craft, when so congregated in a lodge, by a Master and two Wardens, is also a Landmark. The presence of a Master and two Wardens is as essential to the valid organization of a lodge as a warrant of constitution is at the present day. The names, of course, vary in different languages, the Master, for instance, being called "Venerable" in French Masonry, and the Wardens "Surveillants," but the officers, their number, prerogatives and duties, are everywhere identical.

Landmark Eleventh.

The necessity that every lodge, when congregated, should be duly tiled, is an important Landmark of the institution, which is never neglected. The necessity of this law arises from the esoteric character of Masonry. As a secret institution, its portals must of course be guarded from the intrusion of the profane, and such a law must therefore always have been in force from the very beginning of the Order. It is therefore properly classed among the most ancient Landmarks.

Landmark Twelfth.

The right of every Mason to be represented in all general meetings of the craft, and to instruct his representatives, is a twelfth Landmark. Formerly, these general meetings, which were usually held once a year, were called "General Assemblies," and all the fraternity, even to the youngest Entered Apprentice, were permitted to be present. Now they are called "Grand Lodges," and only the Masters and Wardens of the subordinate lodges are summoned. But this is simply as the representatives of their members.

Landmark Thirteenth.

The right of every Mason to appeal from the decision of his brethren in lodge convened, to the Grand Lodge or General Assembly of Masons, is a Landmark highly essential to the preservation of justice, and the prevention of oppression. A few modern Grand Lodges, in adopting a regulation that the decision of subordinate lodges, in cases of expulsion, cannot be wholly set aside upon an appeal, have violated this unquestioned Landmark, as well as the principles of just government.

Landmark Fourteenth.

The right of every Mason to visit and sit in every regular lodge is an unquestionable Landmark of the

Order. This is called "the right of visitation." This right of visitation has always been recognized as an inherent right, which inures to every Mason as he travels through the world. And this is because lodges are justly considered as only divisions for convenience of the universal Masonic family. This right may, of course, be impaired or forfeited on special occasions by various circumstances; but when admission is refused to a Mason in good standing, who knocks at the door of a lodge as a visitor, it is to be expected that some good and sufficient reason shall be furnished for this violation of what is in general a Masonic right, founded on the Landmarks of the Order.

Landmark Fifteenth.

It is a Landmark of the Order, that no visitor, unknown to the brethren present, or to some one of them as a Mason, can enter a lodge without first passing an examination according to ancient usage. Of course, if the visitor is known to any brother present to be a Mason in good standing, and if that brother will vouch for his qualifications, the examination may be dispensed with; as the Landmark refers only to the cases of strangers, who are not to be recognized unless after strict trial, due examination, or lawful information.

Landmark Sixteenth.

No lodge can interfere in the business of another lodge, nor give degrees to brethren who are members of other lodges.

Landmark Seventeenth.

It is a Landmark that every Freemason is amenable to the laws and regulations of the Masonic jurisdiction in which he resides, and this although he may not be a member of any lodge. Non-affiliation does not exempt a Mason from Masonic jurisdiction.

Landmark Eighteenth.

Certain qualifications of candidates for initiation are derived from a Landmark of the Order. These qualifications are that he shall be a man—shall be unmutilated, free born, and of mature age. That is to say, a woman, a cripple, or a slave, or one born in slavery, is disqualified for initiation into the rites of Masonry.

Landmark Nineteenth.

A belief in the existence of God as the Grand Architect of the universe, is one of the most important Landmarks of the Order. It has been always deemed essential that a denial of the existence of a Supreme and Superintending Power, is an absolute disqualification for initiation.

Landmark Twentieth.

Subsidiary to this belief in God, as a Landmark of the Order, is the belief in a resurrection to a future life. This Landmark is not so positively impressed on the candidate by exact words as the preceding; but the doctrine is taught by very plain implication, and runs through the whole symbolism of the Order.

Landmark Twenty-first.

It is a Landmark, that a "Book of the Law" shall constitute an indispensable part of the furniture of every lodge.

Landmark Twenty-second.

The equality of all Masons is another Landmark of the Order. This equality has no reference to any subversion of those gradations of rank which have been instituted by the usages of society. But the doctrine of Masonic equality implies that, as children of one great Father, we meet in the lodge upon the level. When the labors of the lodge are over, and the brethren have retired from their peaceful retreat, to mingle once more with the world, each will then again resume that social position, and exercise the privileges of that rank, to which the customs of society entitle him.

Landmark Twenty-third.

The secrecy of the institution is another and a most important Landmark. Whatever objections may, therefore, be made to the institution, on account of its secrecy, and however much some unskillful brethren have been willing in times of trial, for the sake of expediency, to divest it of its secret character, it will be ever impossible to do so, even were the Landmark not standing before us as an insurmountable obstacle; because such change of its character would be social suicide, and the death of the Order would follow its legalized exposure. Freemasonry, as a secret association, has lived unchanged for centuries —as an open society it would not last for as many years.

Landmark Twenty-fourth.

The foundation of a speculative science upon an operative art, and the symbolic use and explanations of the terms of that art, for purposes of religious or moral teaching, constitute another Landmark of the Order.

Landmark Twenty-fifth.

The last and crowning Landmark of all is, that these Landmarks can never be changed. Nothing can be subtracted from them—nothing can be added to them—not the slightest modification can be made in them.

ANCIENT CONSTITUTIONS.

THE OLD YORK CONSTITUTIONS OF 926.

The Fifteen Articles.

1. The Master must be steadfast, trusty and true; provide victuals for his men, and pay their wages punctually.

2. Every Master shall attend the Grand Lodge when duly summoned, unless he have a good and reasonable excuse.

3. No Master shall take an Apprentice for less than seven years.

4. The son of a bondman shall not be admitted as an Apprentice, lest when he is introduced into the lodge any of the brethren should be offended.

5. A candidate must be without blemish, and have the full and proper use of his limbs; for a maimed man can do the craft no good.

6. The Master shall take especial care, in the admission of an Apprentice, that he do his lord no prejudice.

7. He shall harbor no thief or thief's retainer, lest the craft should come to shame.

8. If he unknowingly employ an imperfect man, he shall discharge him from the work when his inability is discovered.

9. No Master shall undertake a work that he is not able to finish to his lord's profit and the credit of his lodge.

10. A brother shall not supplant his fellow in the work, unless he be incapable of doing it himself; for then he may lawfully finish it, that pleasure and profit may be the mutual result.

11. A Mason shall not be obliged to work after the sun has set in the west.

12. Nor shall he decry the work of a brother or fellow, but shall deal honestly and truly by him, under a penalty of not less than ten pounds.

13. The Master shall instruct his Apprentice faithfully, and make him a perfect workman.

14. He shall teach him all the secrets of his trade,

15. And shall guard him against the commission of perjury, and all other offenses by which the craft may be brought to shame.

The Fifteen Points.

1. Every Mason shall cultivate brotherly love and the love of God, and frequent holy church.

2. The workman shall labor diligently on work days, that he may deserve his holidays.

3. Every Apprentice shall keep his Master's counsel, and not betray the secrets of his lodge.

4. No man shall be false to the craft, or entertain prejudice against his Master or fellows.

5. Every workman shall receive his wages weekly, and without scruple; and should the Master think

proper to dismiss him from the work, he shall have due notice of the same before H. xii.

6. If any dispute arise among the brethren it shall be settled on a holiday, that the work be not neglected, and God's law fulfilled.

7. No Mason shall debauch, or have carnal knowledge of the wife, daughter, or concubine of his Master or fellows.

8. He shall be true to his Master, and a just mediator in all disputes or quarrels.

9. The Steward shall provide good cheer against the hour of refreshment, and each fellow shall punctually defray his share of the reckoning, the Steward rendering a true and correct account.

10. If a Mason live amiss, or slander his brother, so as to bring the craft to shame, he shall have no further maintenance among the brethren, but shall be summoned to the next Grand Lodge; and if he refuse to appear, he shall be expelled.

11. If a brother see his fellow hewing a stone, and likely to spoil it by unskillful workmanship, he shall teach him to amend it, with fair words and brotherly speeches.

12. The General Assembly, or Grand Lodge, shall consist of Master and Fellows, Lords, Knights and Squires, Mayor and Sheriff, to make new laws, and to confirm old ones when necessary.

13. Every brother shall swear fealty, and if he violate his oath, he shall not be succored or assisted by any of the fraternity.

14. He shall make oath to keep secrets, to be steadfast and true to all the ordinances of the Grand Lodge, to the King and Holy Church, and to all the several points herein specified.

15. And if any brother break his oath, he shall be committed to prison, and forfeit his goods and chattels to the King.

They conclude as follows:

That a General Assembly shall be held every year, with the Grand Master at its head, to enforce these regulations, and to make new laws, when it may be expedient to do so, at which all the brethren are competent to be present; and they must renew their O. B. to keep these statutes and constitutions, which have been ordained by King Athelstan, and adopted by the Grand Lodge at York. And this Assembly further directs that, in all ages to come, the existing Grand Lodge shall petition the reigning monarch to confer his sanction on their proceedings.

THE CONSTITUTIONS OF EDWARD III.—1327–1377.

1. That for the future, at the making or admission of a brother, the constitutions and the charges shall be read.

2. That Master Masons, or Masters of the work, shall be examined whether they be able of cunning to serve their respective lords, as well the highest as the lowest, to the honor and worship of the aforesaid art, and to the profit of their lords; for they be their lords that employ them for their travel.

3. That when the Master and Wardens meet in a lodge, if need be, the sheriff of the county, or the mayor of the city, or alderman of the town, in which the congregation is held, should be made fellow and sociate to the Master, in help of him against rebels, and for upbearing the rights of the realm.

4. That Entered Prentices at their making were charged not to be thieves, or thieves-maintainers; that they should travel honestly for their pay, and love their Fellows as themselves, and be true to the King of England, and to the realm, and to the Lodge.

5. That at such congregations it shall be enquired, whether any Master or Fellow has broken any of the

articles agreed to. And if the offender, being duly cited to appear, prove rebel, and will not attend, then the Lodge shall determine against him that he shall forswear (or renounce) his Masonry, and shall no more use this Craft; the which, if he presume for to do, the Sheriff of the county shall prison him, and take all his goods into the king's hands, till his grace be granted him an issue: for this cause principally have these congregations been ordained, that as well the lowest as the highest should be well and truly served in this art foresaid throughout all the kingdom of England.

REGULATIONS OF 1663.

1. That no person, of what degree soever, be made or accepted a Freemason, unless in a regular Lodge, whereof one to be a Master or Warden in that limit or division where such lodge is kept, and another to be a craftsman in the trade of Freemasonry.

2. That no person shall hereafter be accepted a Freemason but such as are of able body, honest parentage, good reputation, and an observer of the laws of the land.

3. That no person hereafter who shall be accepted a Freemason shall be admitted into any lodge or assembly, until he has brought a certificate of the time and place of his acceptation from the lodge that accepted him, unto the Master of that limit or division where such lodge is kept; and the said Master shall enroll the same in a roll of parchment, to be kept for that purpose, and shall give an account of all such acceptations at every General Assembly.

4. That every person who is now a Freemason shall bring to the Master a note of the time of his acceptation, to the end the same may be enrolled in such priority of place as the brother deserves; and that

the whole company and Fellows may the better know each other.

5. That for the future the said fraternity of Freemasons shall be regulated and governed by one Grand Master, and as many Wardens as the said society shall think fit to appoint at every annual General Assembly.

6. That no person shall be accepted, unless he be twenty-one years old or more.

THE ANCIENT INSTALLATION CHARGES OF JAMES II. 1685–'88.

1. That ye shall be true men to God and the Holy Church, and to use no error or heresy by your understanding, and by wise men's teaching.

2. That ye shall be true liegemen to the King of England, without treason or any falsehood, and that ye know no treason but ye shall give knowledge thereof to the king, or to his counsel; also, ye shall be true one to another, that is to say, every Mason of the craft that is Mason allowed, ye shall do to him as ye would be done unto yourself.

3. And ye shall keep truly all the counsel that ought to be kept in the way of Masonhood, and all the counsel of the Lodge or of the chamber. Also, that ye shall be no thief, nor thieves to your knowledge free; that ye shall be true to the king, lord or master that ye serve, and truly see and work for his advantage.

4. Ye shall call all Masons your Fellows, or your brethren, and no other names.

5. Ye shall not take your Fellow's wife in villainy, nor deflower his daughter or servant, nor put him to disworship.

6. Ye shall truly pay for meat or drink, wheresoever ye go to table or board. Also, ye shall do no

villainy there, whereby the craft or science may be slandered.

THE ANCIENT CHARGES AT MAKINGS.

1. That a Mason take on him no lord's work, nor any other man's, unless he know himself well able to perform the work, so that the craft have no slander.

2. Also, that no Master take work but that he take reasonable pay for it; so that the lord may be truly served, and the Master to live honestly, and to pay his Fellows truly. And that no Master or Fellow supplant others of their work; that is to say, that if he hath taken a work, or else stand Master of any work, that he shall not put him out, unless he be unable of cunning to make an end of his work. And no Master nor Fellow shall take an Apprentice for less than seven years. And that the Apprentice be freeborn, and of limbs whole as a man ought to be, and no bastard. And that no Master nor Fellow take no allowance to be made Mason without the assent of his Fellows, at the least six or seven.

3. That he that be made be able in all degrees; that is, free born, of a good kindred, true, and no bondsman, and that he have his right limbs as a man ought to have.

4. That a Master take no Apprentice without he have occupation to occupy two or three Fellows at least.

5. That no Master or Fellow put away any lord's work to task that ought to be journeywork.

6. That every Master give pay to his Fellows and servants as they may deserve, so that he be not defamed with false working. And that none shall slander another behind his back to make him lose his good name.

7. That no Fellow in the house or abroad answer another ungodly or reproveably without a cause.

8. That every Master Mason do reverence to his elder; and that a Mason be no common player at the cards, dice or hazard; or at any unlawful plays, through the which the science and craft may be dishonored and slandered.

9. That no Fellow go into the town by night, except he have a Fellow with him, who may bear him record that he was in an honest place.

10. That every Master and Fellow shall come to the assembly, if it be within fifty miles of him, if he have any warning. And if he have trespassed against the craft, to abide the reward of Masters and Fellows.

11. That every Master Mason and Fellow that hath trespassed against the craft shall stand to the correction of other Masters and Fellows to make him accord; and if they cannot accord, to go to the common law.

12. That a Master or Fellow make not a mould stone, square nor rule, to no lowen, nor let no lowen work within their lodge nor without, to mould stone.

13. That every Mason receive and cherish strange Fellows, when they come over the country, and set them on work, if they will work, as the manner is; that is to say, if the Mason have any mould stone in his place, he shall give him a mould stone, and set him on work; and if he have none, the Mason shall refresh him with money until the next lodge.

14. That every Mason shall truly serve his Master for his pay.

15. That every Master shall truly make an end of his work, task or journey, whither so it be.

THE CHARGES OF A FREEMASON.

Extracted from the Ancient Records of Lodges beyond Sea, and of those in England, Scotland and Ireland, for the use of the Lodges in London. To be read at the making of New Brethren, or when the Master shall order it.

I.—CONCERNING GOD AND RELIGION.

A Mason is obliged, by his tenure, to obey the moral law; and if he rightly understands the Art, he will never be a stupid Atheist, nor an irreligious Libertine. But though in ancient times Masons were charged in every country to be of the religion of that country or nation, whatever it was; it is now thought more expedient only to oblige them to that religion in which all men agree, leaving their particular opinions to themselves; that is, to be *good men and true*, or men of honor and honesty, by whatever denominations or persuasions they may be distinguished; whereby Masonry becomes the *Center* of *Union*, and the means of conciliating true friendship among persons that must have remained at a perpetual distance.

II.—OF THE CIVIL MAGISTRATE, SUPREME AND SUBORDINATE.

A Mason is a peaceable subject to the civil powers wherever he resides or works, and is never to be concerned in plots and conspiracies against the peace and welfare of the nation, nor to behave himself undutifully to inferior magistrates; for as Masonry hath been always injured by war, bloodshed, and confusion, so ancient kings and princes have been much disposed to encourage the craftsmen, because of their peaceableness and loyalty, whereby they practically answered the cavils of their adversaries, and promoted the honor of the Fraternity, who ever flourished in times of peace. So that if a brother should be a rebel against the State, he is not to be countenanced in his rebellion, however he may be pitied as an unhappy man; and if convicted of no other crime, though the loyal brotherhood must and ought to disown his rebellion, and give no umbrage or ground of political jealousy to the government for the time being, they cannot expel him from the lodge, and his relation to it remains indefeasible.

III.—OF LODGES.

A lodge is a place where Masons assemble and work: Hence that Assembly, or duly organized Society of Masons, is called a *Lodge*, and every brother ought to belong to one, and to be subject to its By Laws and the General Regulations. It is either particular or general, and will be best understood by attending it, and by the regulations of the General or Grand Lodge hereunto annexed. In ancient times, no Master or Fellow could be absent from it, especially when warned to appear at it, without incurring a severe censure, until it appeared to the Master and Wardens that pure necessity hindered him.

The persons admitted members of a lodge must be good and true men, free-born, and of mature and discreet age; no bondmen, no women, no immoral or scandalous men, but of good report.

IV.—OF MASTERS, WARDENS, FELLOWS AND APPRENTICES.

All preferment among Masons is grounded upon real worth and personal merit only; that so the lords may be well served, the brethren not put to shame, nor the Royal Craft despised: Therefore no Master or Warden is chosen by seniority, but for his merit. It is impossible to describe these things in writing, and every brother must attend in his place, and learn them in a way peculiar to this Fraternity: Only candidates may know that no Master should take an Apprentice, unless he has sufficient employment for him, and unless he be a perfect youth, having no maim or defect in his body, that may render him incapable of learning the art of serving his master's LORD, and of being made a *Brother*, and then a *Fellow Craft* in due time, even after he has served such a term of years as the custom of the country directs; and that he should be descended of honest parents; that so, when otherwise qualified, he may arrive to the honor of being the *Warden*, and then the *Master* of the lodge, the *Grand Warden*, and at length the *Grand Master* of all the lodges, according to his merit.

No brother can be a Warden until he has passed the part of a Fellow Craft; nor a Master until he has acted as a Warden, nor Grand Warden until he has been Master of a lodge, nor Grand Master, unless he has been a Fellow Craft before his election, who is also to be nobly born, or a gentleman of the best fashion, or some eminent scholar, or some curious architect or other artist, descended of honest parents, and who is of singular great merit in the opinion of the lodges. And for the better, and easier, and more honorable discharge of his office, the Grand Master has a power to choose his own Deputy Grand Master, who must be then, or must have been formerly, the Master of a particular lodge, and has the privilege of acting whatever the Grand Master, his Principal, should act, unless the said Principal be present, or interpose his authority by a letter.

These rulers and governors—supreme and subordinate—of the ancient lodge, are to be obeyed in their respective stations by all the brethren, according to the old Charges and Regulations, with all humility, reverence, love and alacrity.

V.—OF THE MANAGEMENT OF THE CRAFT IN WORKING.

All Masons shall work honestly on working days, that they may live creditably on holy days; and the time appointed by the law of the land, or confirmed by custom, shall be observed.

The most expert of the Fellow Craftsmen shall be chosen or appointed the Master or overseer of the lord's work: who is to be called Master by those that work under him. The craftsmen are to avoid all ill language, and to call each other by no disobliging name, but Brother or Fellow; and to behave themselves courteously within and without the lodge.

The Master, knowing himself to be able of cunning, shall undertake the lord's work as reasonably as possible, and truly dispend his goods as if they were his own; nor to give more wages to any Brother or Apprentice than he really may deserve.

Both the Master and the Mason receiving their wages justly, shall be faithful to the lord, and honestly finish their work, whether task or journey: nor put the work to task that hath been accustomed to journey.

None shall discover envy at the prosperity of a Brother, nor supplant him, or put him out of his work, if he be capable to finish the same: for no man can finish another's work so much to the lord's profit, unless he be thoroughly acquainted with the designs and draughts of him that began it.

When a Fellow Craftsman is chosen Warden of the work under the Master, he shall be true both to Master and Fellows; shall carefully oversee the work in the Master's absence to the lord's profit; and his brethren shall obey him.

All Masons employed shall meekly receive their wages without murmuring or mutiny, and not desert the Master till the work is finished.

A younger brother shall be instructed in working, to prevent spoiling the materials for want of judgment, and for increasing and continuing of brotherly love.

All the tools used in working shall be approved by the Grand Lodge.

No laborer shall be employed in the proper work of Masonry; nor shall Free Masons work with those that are not free, without an urgent necessity; nor shall they teach laborers and unaccepted Masons, as they should teach a Brother or Fellow.

VI.—OF BEHAVIOR, VIZ:

1. *In the Lodge while Constituted.*

You are not to hold private committees, or separate conversation, without leave from the Master, nor to talk of anything impertinent or unseemly, nor interrupt the Master or Wardens, or any brother speaking to the Master; nor behave yourself ludicrously or jestingly while the lodge is engaged in what is serious and solemn; nor use any unbecoming language upon any pretence whatsoever; but to pay due reverence to your Master, Wardens and Fellows, and put them to worship.

If any complaint be brought, the brother found guilty shall stand to the award and determination of the lodge, who are the proper and competent judges of all such controversies, (unless you carry it by appeal to the Grand Lodge,) and to whom they ought to be referred, unless a lord's work be hindered the meanwhile, in which case a particular reference may be made; but you must never go to law about what concerneth Masonry, without an absolute necessity apparent to the Lodge.

2. *Behavior after the Lodge is over and the Brethren not gone.*

You may enjoy yourselves with innocent mirth, treating one another according to ability, but avoiding all excess, or forcing any brother to eat or drink beyond his inclination, or hindering him from going when his occasions call him, or doing or saying any thing offensive, or that may forbid an easy and free conversation; for that would blast our harmony and defeat our laudable purposes. Therefore no private piques or quarrels must be brought within the door of the lodge, far less any quarrels about religion, or nations, or state policy, we being only, as Masons, of the Catholic religion above mentioned; we are also of all nations, tongues, kindreds, and languages, and are resolved against all politics, as what never yet conduced to the welfare of the lodge, nor ever will. This Charge has always been strictly enjoined and observed; but especially ever since the reformation in Britain, or the dissent and secession of those nations from the communion of Rome.

3. *Behavior when Brethren meet without Strangers, but not in a Lodge formed.*

You are to salute one another in a courteous manner, as you will be instructed, calling each other BROTHER, freely giving mutual instruction, as shall be thought expedient, without being overseen or overheard, and without encroaching upon each other, or derogating from that respect which is due any brother, were he not a Mason; for though all Masons are as brethren upon the same level, yet Masonry takes no honor from a man that he had before; nay, rather it adds to his honor, especially if he has deserved well of the brotherhood, who must give honor to whom it is due, and avoid ill manners.

4. *Behavior in Presence of Strangers not Masons.*

You shall be cautious in your words and carriage, that the most penetrating stranger shall not be able to discover or find out what is not proper to be intimated; and sometimes you shall divert a discourse, and manage it prudently for the honor of the Worshipful Fraternity.

5. *Behavior at Home and in your Neighborhood.*

You are to act as becomes a moral and wise man, particularly not to let your family, friends and neighbors know the concerns of the lodge, etc., but wisely to consult your own honor, and that of the Ancient Brotherhood, for reasons not to be mentioned here. You must also consult your health, by not continuing together too late, or too long from home, after lodge hours are past; and by avoiding of gluttony or drunkenness, that your families be not neglected or injured, nor you disabled from working.

6. *Behavior toward a Strange Brother.*

You are cautiously to examine him, in such a method as prudence shall direct you, that you may not be imposed upon by an ignorant false pretender, whom you are to reject with contempt and derision, and beware of giving him any hints of your knowledge.

But if you discover him to be a true and genuine brother, you are to respect him accordingly; and if he is in want, you must relieve him, if you can, or else direct him how he may be relieved: You must employ him some days, or else recommend him to be employed. But you are not charged to do beyond your ability, only to prefer a poor brother, that is a good man and true, before any other people in the same circumstances.

Finally. All these CHARGES you are to observe, and also those that shall be communicated to you in another way; cultivating brotherly love, the foundation and cap-stone, the cement and glory of this ancient fraternity; avoiding all wrangling and quarreling, all slander and backbiting, nor permitting others to slander any honest brother, but defending his character, and doing him all good offices, as far as is consistent with your honor and safety, and no farther. And if any of them do you injury, you must apply to your own or his lodge, and from thence you may appeal to the Grand Lodge at the Quarterly Communication, and from thence to the Annual Grand Lodge, as has been the ancient laudable conduct of our forefathers in every nation; never taking a legal course, but when the case cannot be otherwise decided, and patiently listening to the honest and friendly advice of Master and fellows, when they would prevent your going to law with strangers, or would excite you to put a period to all lawsuits, that so you may mind the affair of Masonry with the more alacrity and success; but with respect to brothers or fellows at law, the Master and brethren should kindly offer their mediation, which ought to be thankfully submitted to by the contending brethren; and if that submission is impracticable, they must, however, carry on their process, or lawsuit, without wrath and rancor, (not in the common way,) saying or doing nothing which may hinder brotherly love, and good offices to be renewed and continued; that all may see the benign influence of Masonry, as all true Masons have done from the beginning of the world, and will do to the end of time. AMEN. *So mote it be.*

APPENDIX OF GENERAL FORMS.

PETITION FOR DISPENSATION TO FORM A NEW LODGE.

To the M. W. Grand Master of Masons of the State of Michigan.

The undersigned petitioners, being Ancient Free and Accepted Masons, having the prosperity of the fraternity at heart, and being willing to exert their best endeavors to promote and diffuse the genuine principles of Freemasonry, respectfully represent—

That they are desirous of forming a new lodge at ......, in the county of......, State of Michigan, to be named......Lodge. They therefore pray for a warrant or dispensation, to empower them to assemble as a lawful lodge, to discharge the duties of Masonry in the several degrees of Entered Apprentice, Fellow Craft and Master Mason, in a regular and constitutional manner, according to the ancient forms of the fraternity, and the laws and regulations of the Grand Lodge.

They have nominated and do recommend Brother A. B. to be the first Worshipful Master, C. D. to be the first Senior Warden, and E. F. to be the first Junior Warden, of said lodge.

If the prayer of this petition shall be granted, they promise a strict conformity to all the constitutional laws, rules and regulations of the fraternity and of the Grand Lodge.

(This petition must be signed by at least eight Master Masons, one of whom must be of the degree of P. M., and should be filed with the Grand Secretary. For its necessary accompaniments, see Decisions of G. M., No. 73, page 141 of this volume.)

DISPENSATION FOR NEW LODGE.

Grand Lodge of Free and Accepted Masons of the State of Michigan.

To all to whom these presents may come, greeting:

Whereas, a petition has been presented to me, by sundry brethren residing within this jurisdiction, to wit:........., praying, on account of the convenience of their respective dwellings, and for other good reasons, for a dispensation to empower them to assemble as a legal lodge, to discharge the duties of Masonry in the several degrees of Entered Apprentice, Fellow Craft, and Master Mason, in a regular and constitutional manner, according to the ancient forms of the fraternity, and the constitution and regulations of this Grand Lodge, and promising a strict conformity to all constitutional laws, rules and regulations of the same.

And whereas, the said petitioners have been recommended to me as Master Masons in good standing by the Worshipful Master, Wardens and brethren, of ......Lodge, No... under our jurisdiction. Therefore I,......Grand Master of the Grand Lodge of Free and Accepted Masons of the State of Michigan, by virtue of the authority in me vested, do hereby grant this my dispensation, authorizing and empowering our trusty and well beloved brethren aforesaid, to form and open a new lodge, in the......of......in the county of......and State of Michigan, to be called......Lodge, and therein to admit and make Entered Apprentices, Fellow Crafts, and Master Masons, in accordance with the ancient usages and customs of the fraternity, obeying in all things the constitution, laws and edicts of this Grand Lodge, and not otherwise.

And I do hereby appoint our worthy brother A. B. to be the first Master, brother C. D. to be the first Senior Warden, and brother E. F. to be the first Junior Warden, of said new lodge.

And it shall be their duty, and they are hereby required to return this dispensation, with a correct transcript of all proceedings had under the authority of the same, together with an attested copy of their by-laws, to our Grand Lodge, at its next annual communication, for examination, and such further action as shall then be deemed wise and proper.

This dispensation to continue in full force till the annual communication aforesaid, unless sooner revoked by me.

{ Seal of the G. L. } In testimony whereof, I have hereunto set my hand, and affixed the seal of the Grand Lodge, at Detroit, this......day of ......A. D. 18..., A. L. 58...

A...... T...... M......, Grand Master.

Attest:
J...... F......, Grand Secretary.

PROXY FROM THE GRAND MASTER TO CONSTITUTE AND CONSECRATE A NEW LODGE, AND INSTALL OFFICERS.

Office of the Grand Master of Masons of the State of Michigan, ..., 18...

To all whom it may concern—greeting:

Know ye, that reposing full confidence in the skill and Masonic ability of our Worshipful Brother......,

I, Grand Master of the M. W. Grand Lodge of......, do by these presents constitute and appoint him my Proxy, for me and in my name, to constitute and consecrate......Lodge, No..., and to install the officers thereof in due and ancient form, he making due return to me of his doings in the premises.

Given under my hand and private seal, at......, the day and year first above written.

[Private Seal.]

A...... T...... M......, Grand Master.

PETITION FOR DISPENSATION TO CONFER DEGREES ON, OR BALLOT FOR, A CANDIDATE, IN LESS THAN THE REGULAR TIME.

Hall of......Lodge, No...,
......18...

To the M. W. Grand Master of Masons of the State of Michigan.

By a vote of this lodge, I am instructed to ask you for a dispensation to pass the ballot (or confer the degrees, as the case may be) for M. A. B., who has petitioned this lodge for initiation, (or is anxious to receive the degrees of F. C. and M. M., as the case may be,) at a special meeting, to be called for that purpose.

M. A. B. is ... years of age; his residence is...... ; his occupation is...... The case is one of emergency, for the reasons following: [Here state at length the reasons why a dispensation should be granted in the case. See Decisions of G. M., No. 55.]

O...... P......, Worshipful Master.

[Seal of Lodge.]

PETITION FOR INITIATION.

To the Worshipful Master, Wardens and Brethren of......Lodge, No..., of F. and A. Masons.

The petition of the subscriber respectfully showeth, that having long entertained a favorable opinion of your ancient institution, he is desirous of being admitted a member thereof, if found worthy.

His place of residence is......, his age...years, his occupation......

He has......applied for initiation into Masonry heretofore. (If application has ever before been made to any lodge, state when, where, the number of times, to what lodge or lodges, and whether the applicant was elected or rejected. See Res. of G. L., No. 25, page 156 of this volume.)

A...... B......

Recommended by
G...... H......
L...... N......

APPLICATION FOR MEMBERSHIP.

To the Worshipful Master, Wardens and Brethren of......Lodge, No..., of F. and A. Masons.

The petition of the subscriber respectfully showeth that he is a Master Mason of good standing—and residing within the jurisdiction of your lodge, is desirous of being admitted a member thereof, if found worthy.

Accompanying this petition is a dimit from the lodge of which he was last a member, and if received, he promises a strict compliance with the by-laws of the lodge, and the general regulations and usages of Ancient Free Masonry.

E...... F......

Recommended by
A...... B......
C...... D......

DIMIT.

Hall of......Lodge, No... of F. and A. Masons.

Held at......, by authority of the Grand Lodge of Michigan.

I hereby certify that at a......meeting of......Lodge, No..., held on the......day of......, A. L. 58..., Bro. ......, by consent of said lodge, withdrew his membership from the same; he being at the time a Worthy Master Mason in good standing, and having paid all dues assessed against him.

By order of said lodge,

[L. S.] ......, Secretary.

GRAND LODGE CERTIFICATE.

Grand Lodge of Free and Accepted Masons of the State of Michigan.

I hereby certify, that......Lodge, No..., is regularly constituted and held under the authority and jurisdiction of this Grand Lodge, and that A. B. is Worshipful Master, C. D. is Senior Warden, and E. F. is Junior Warden of said lodge.

In testimony whereof, I have hereunto set my hand and affixed the Seal of the Grand Lodge, at Detroit, this......day of......A. L. 58..., A. D. 18...

[Seal of G. L.] J...... F......, Grand Sec'y.

We, the Master and Wardens of......Lodge, No..., held under the authority and jurisdiction of the Grand Lodge of F. and A. Masons of the State of Michigan, do hereby certify that our worthy and well beloved Brother......, (who has written his name below,) is a Master Mason, in good standing in our lodge, and he is hereby recommended to the favor and protection of the Craft throughout the Globe.

Given under our hands and the seal of our Lodge, at......this......day of......, A. L. 58..., A. D. 18...

A...... B......, W. M.
[Seal of the Lodge.] C...... D......, S. W.
E...... F......, J. W.

Attest: G...... H......, Secretary.

Signature of.........

(Application for the above certificate should be made to the Grand Secretary, either verbally or by letter, and should be accompanied by the Constitutional fee.)

REPRESENTATIVE'S CERTIFICATE.

......Lodge, No...

This is to certify that at a communication of...... Lodge, No..., held on the......day of......A. D. 18..., A. L. 58..., our Worthy Brother......was deputed to represent the Worshipful Master of this lodge at the next session of the Grand Lodge of F. and A. Masons of the State of Michigan.

In testimony whereof, I have hereunto set my hand and affixed the Seal of......Lodge, at......this......day of......A. D. 18..., A. L. 58...

........., W. M.

Attest: ...., Secretary.

(See Sec's. 1, 2 and 3 of Art. 2, and Sec. 2 of Art. 6 of Const. of G. L.)

FINIS.

www.ingramcontent.com/pod-product-compliance
Lightning Source LLC
LaVergne TN
LVHW050526100826
845148LV00002B/457

* 9 7 8 1 4 2 5 5 1 9 5 8 2 *